# The St. Patrick's Day Coloring Book



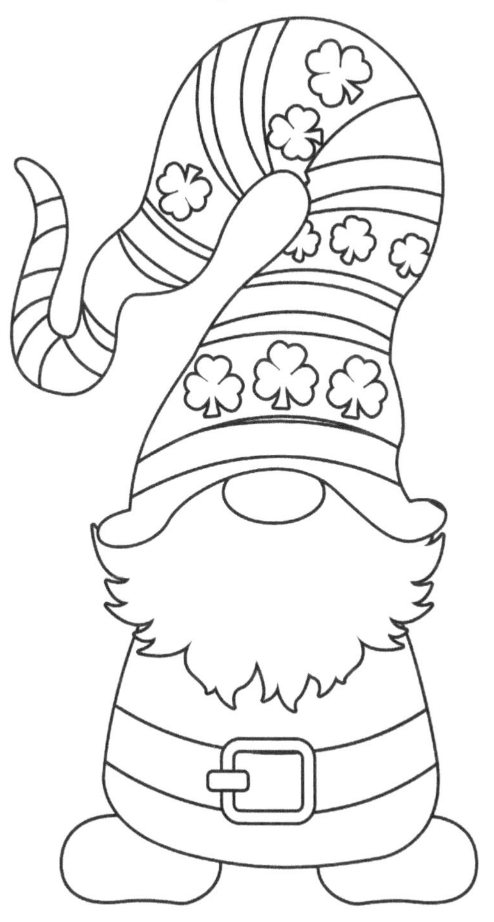

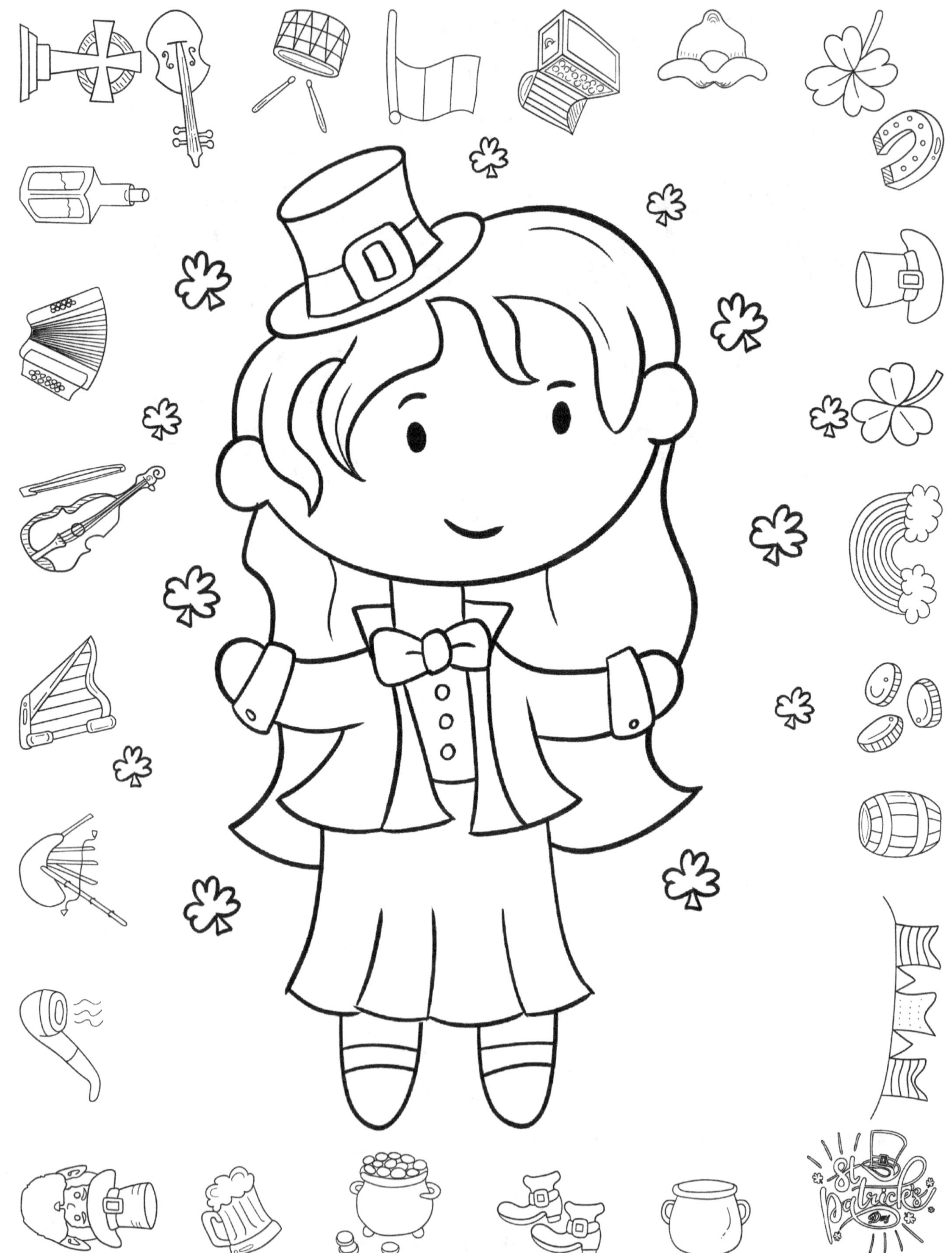
St Patrick's Day

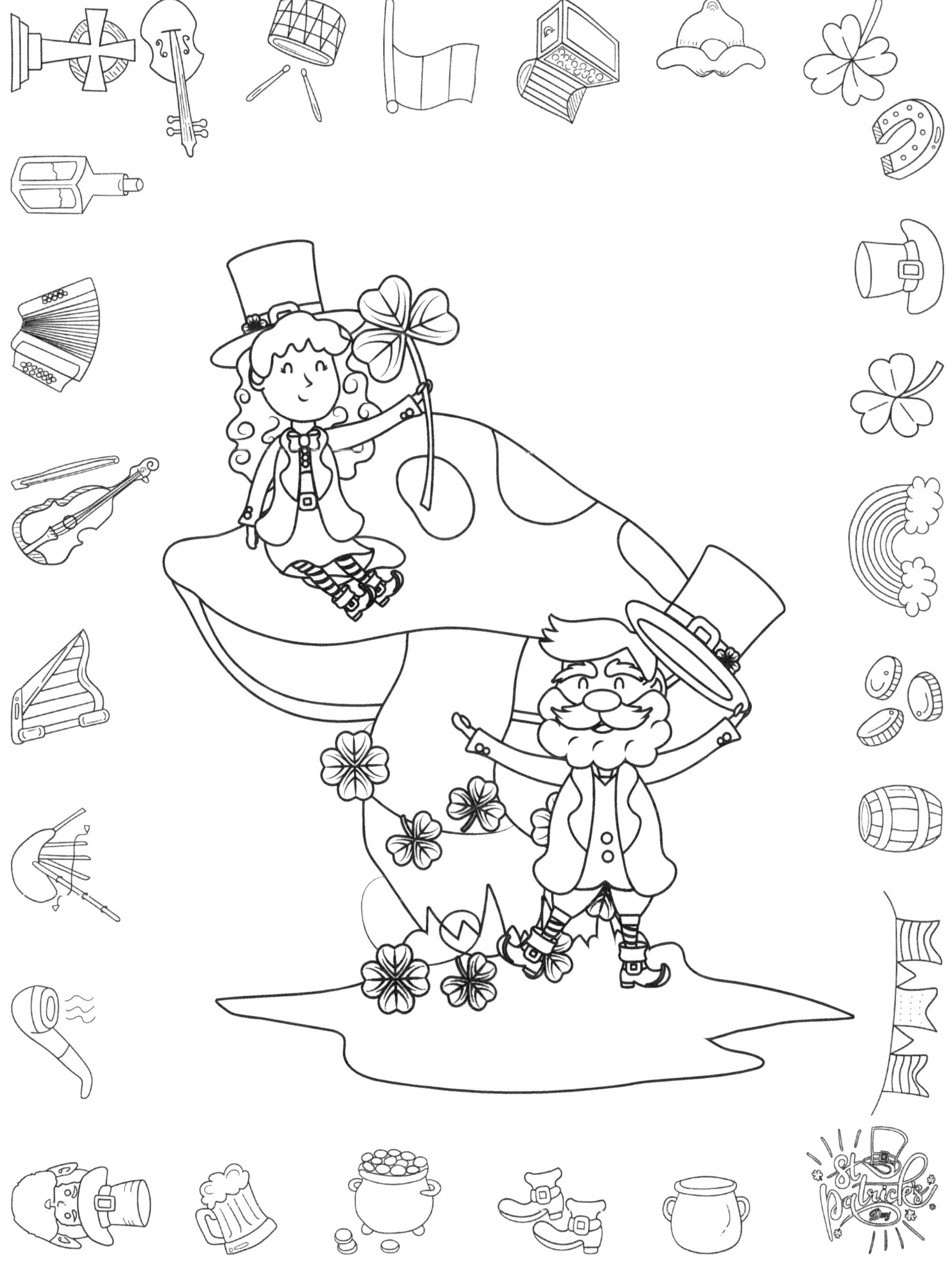

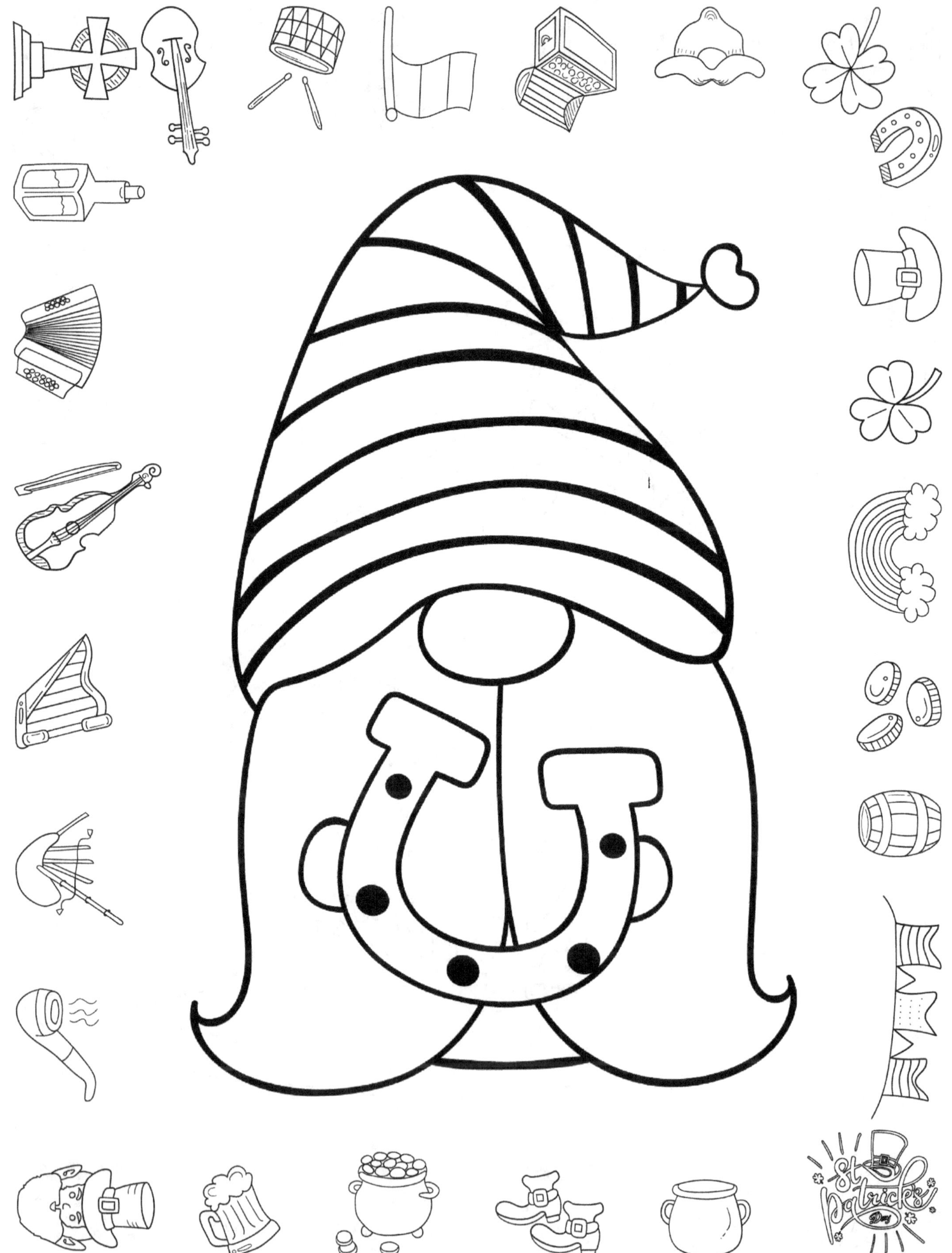

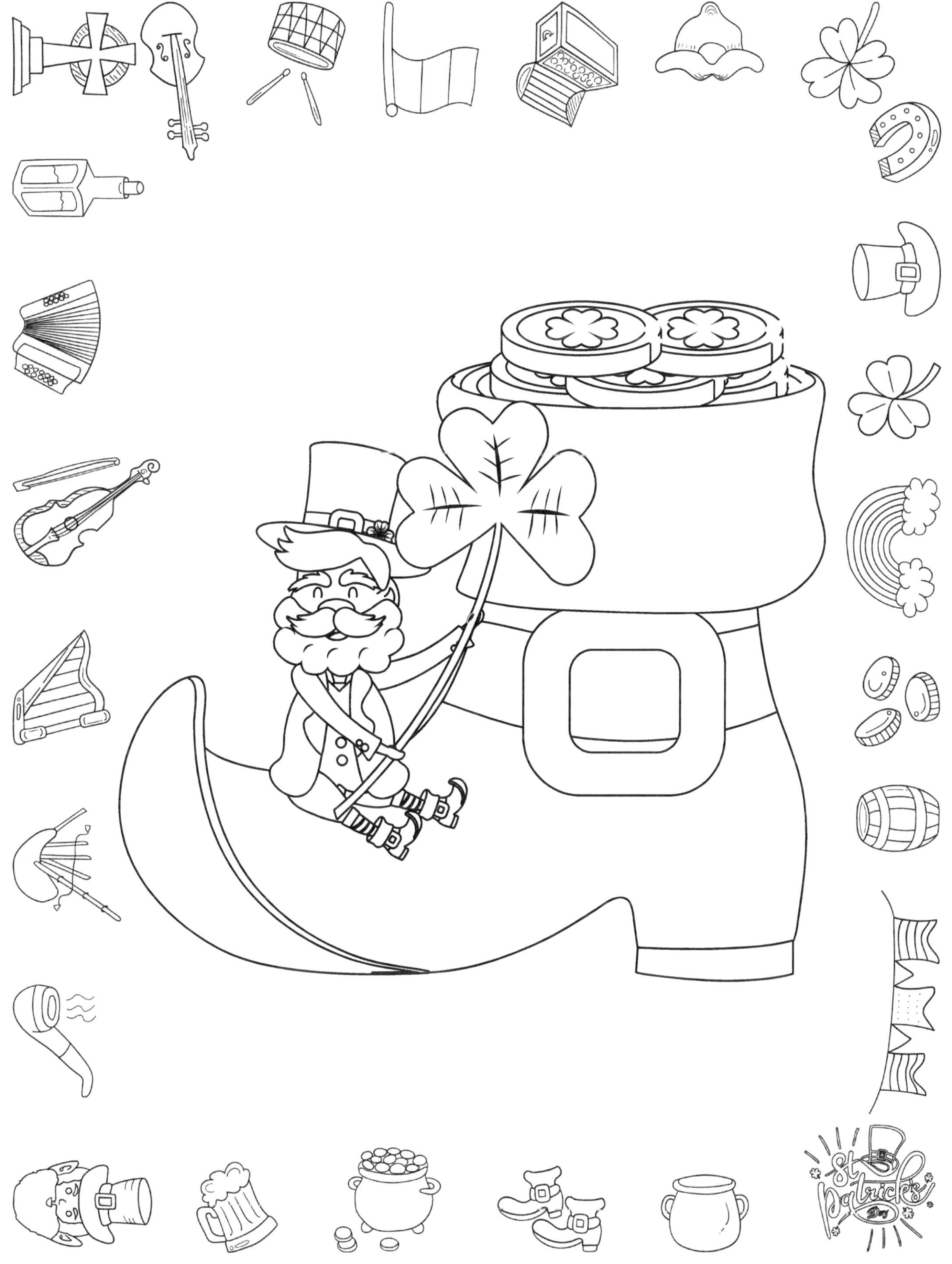

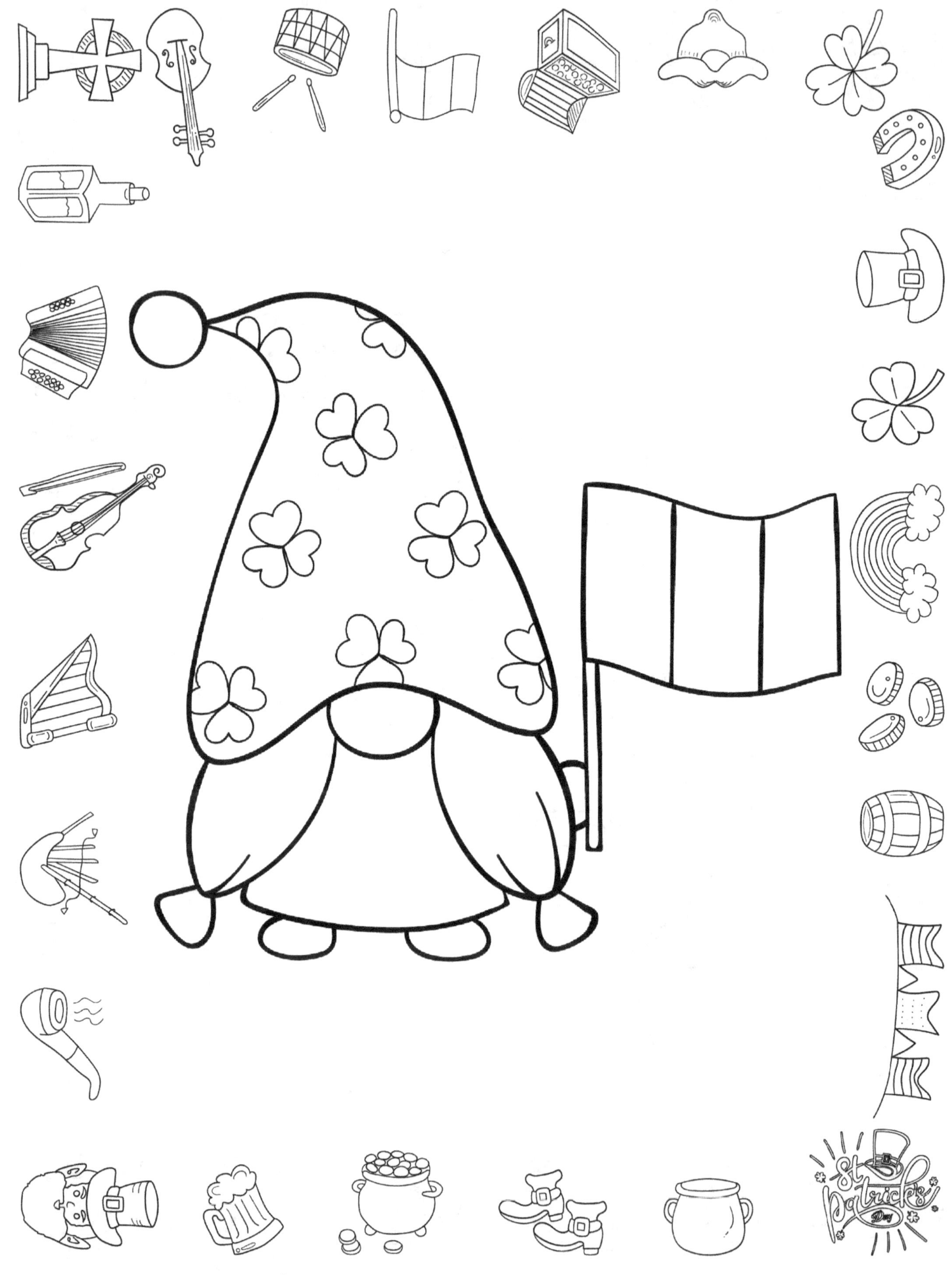

St Patrick's
Day

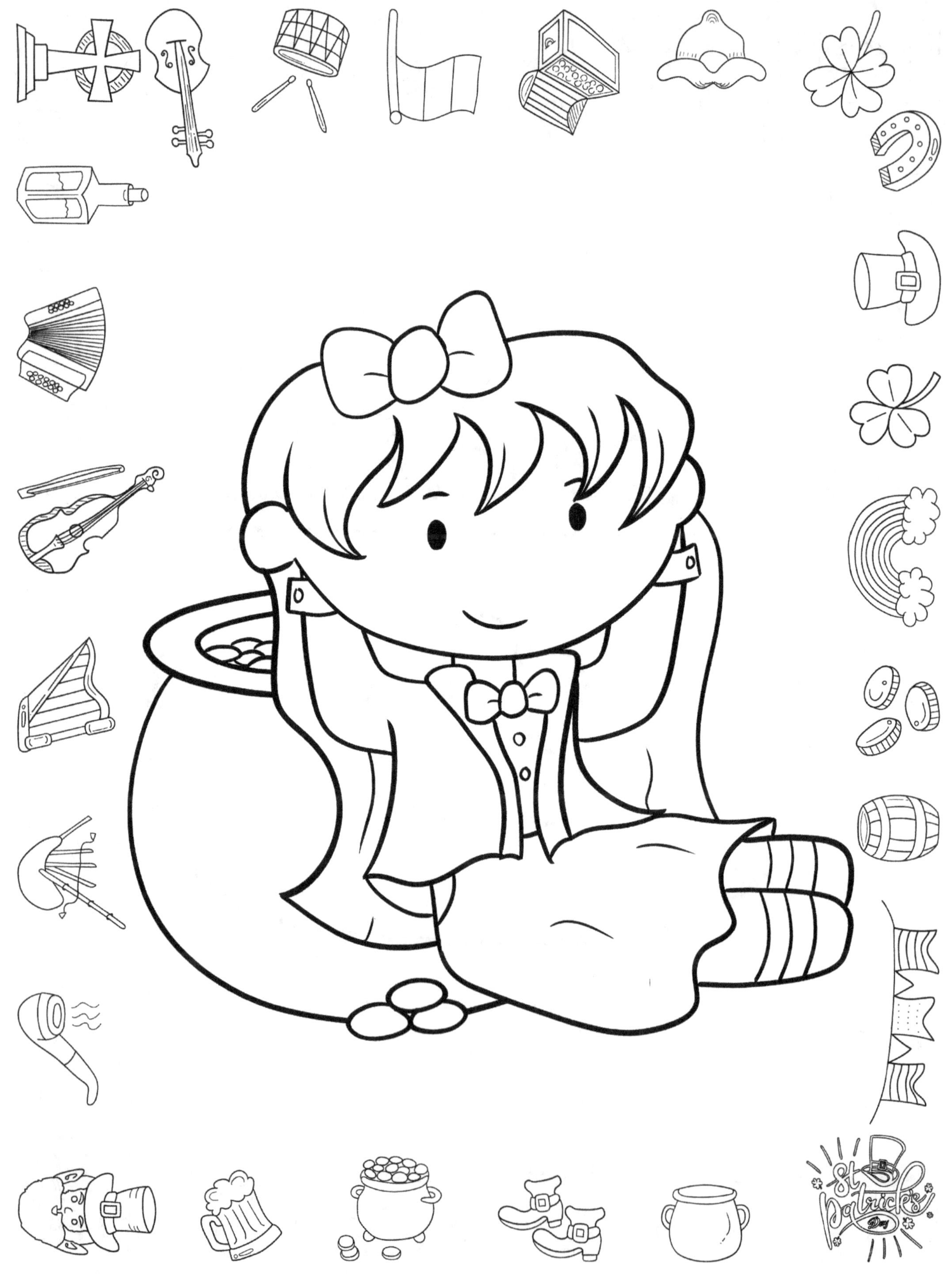

St Patrick's Day

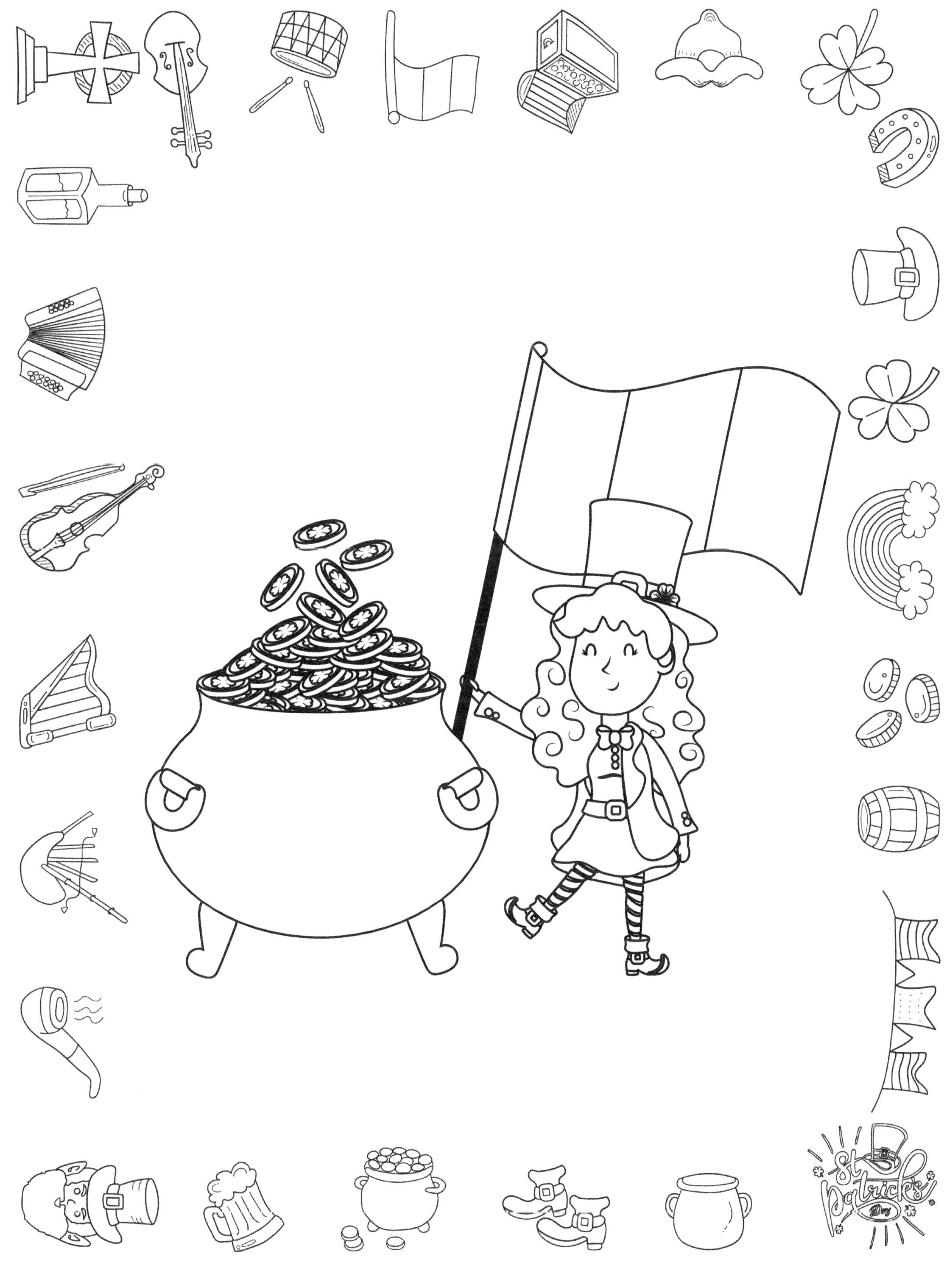

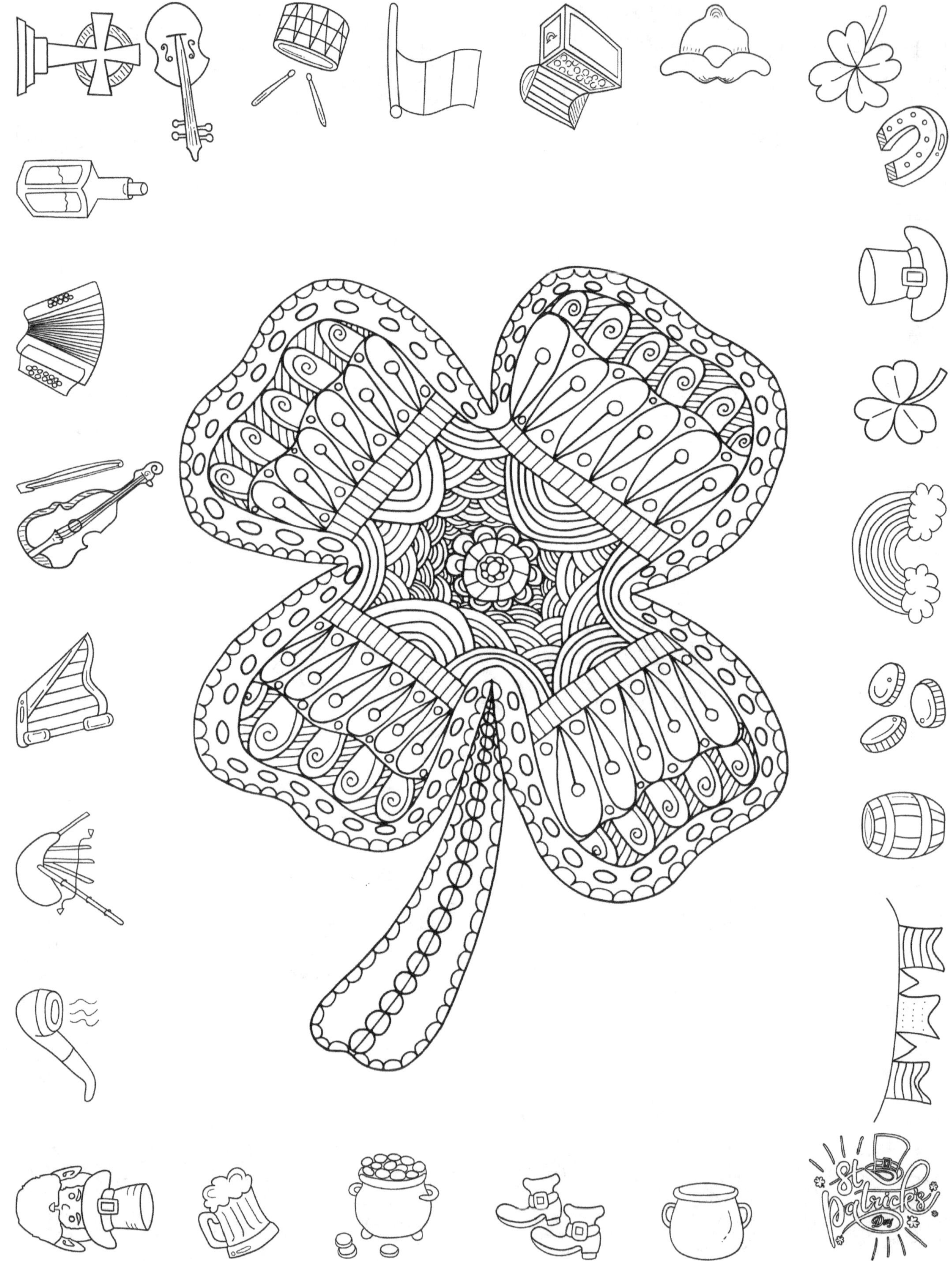

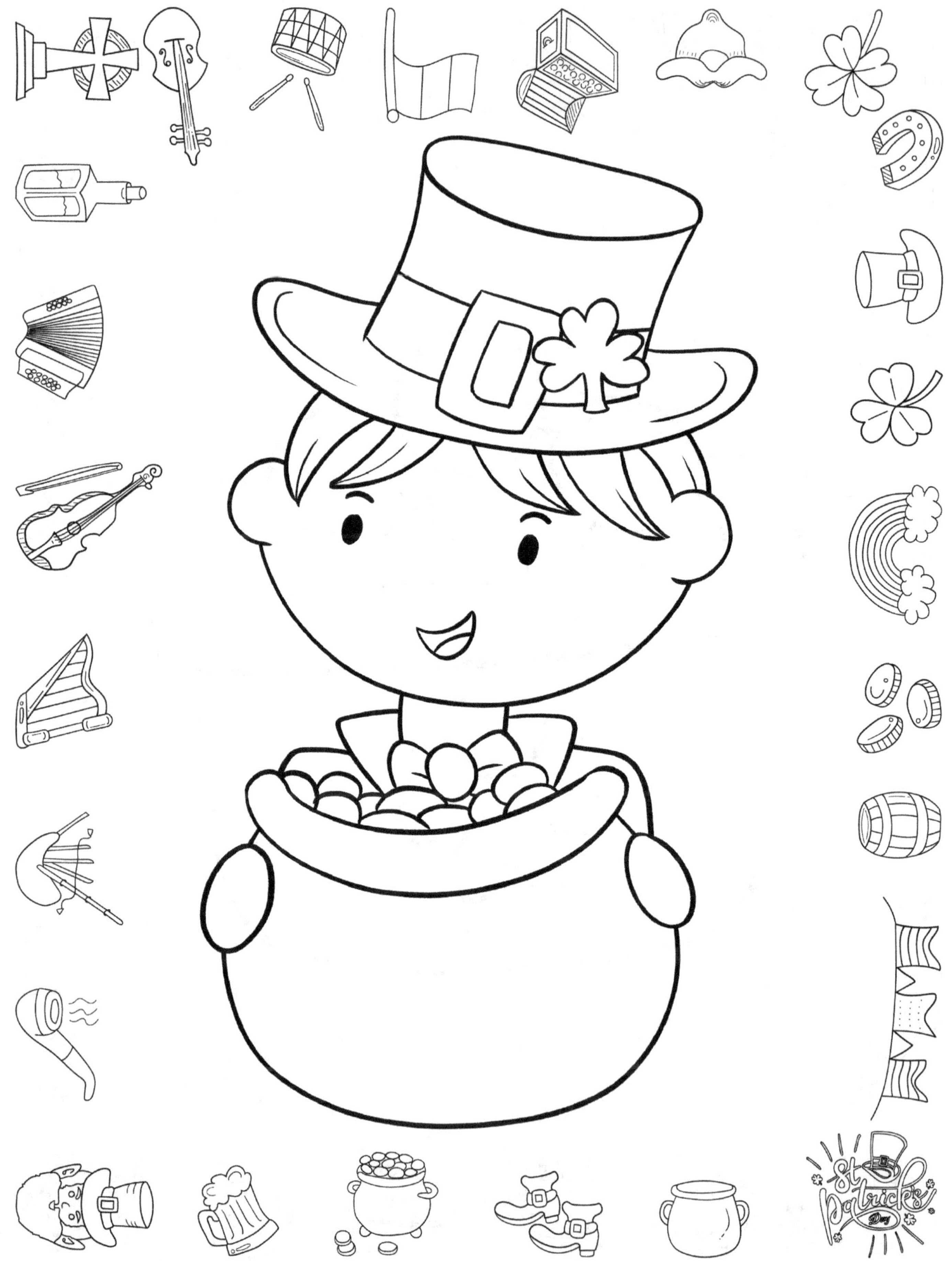

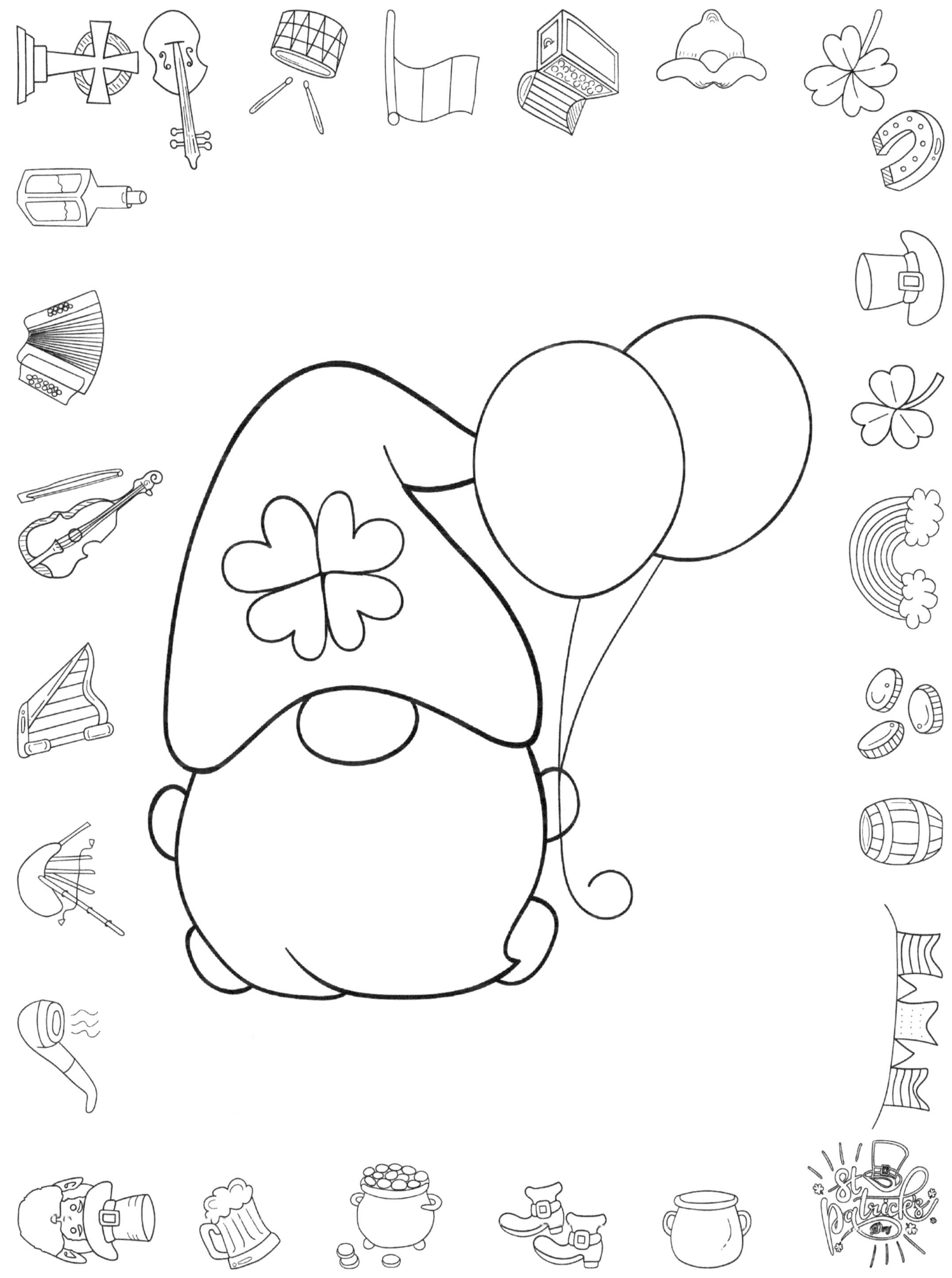

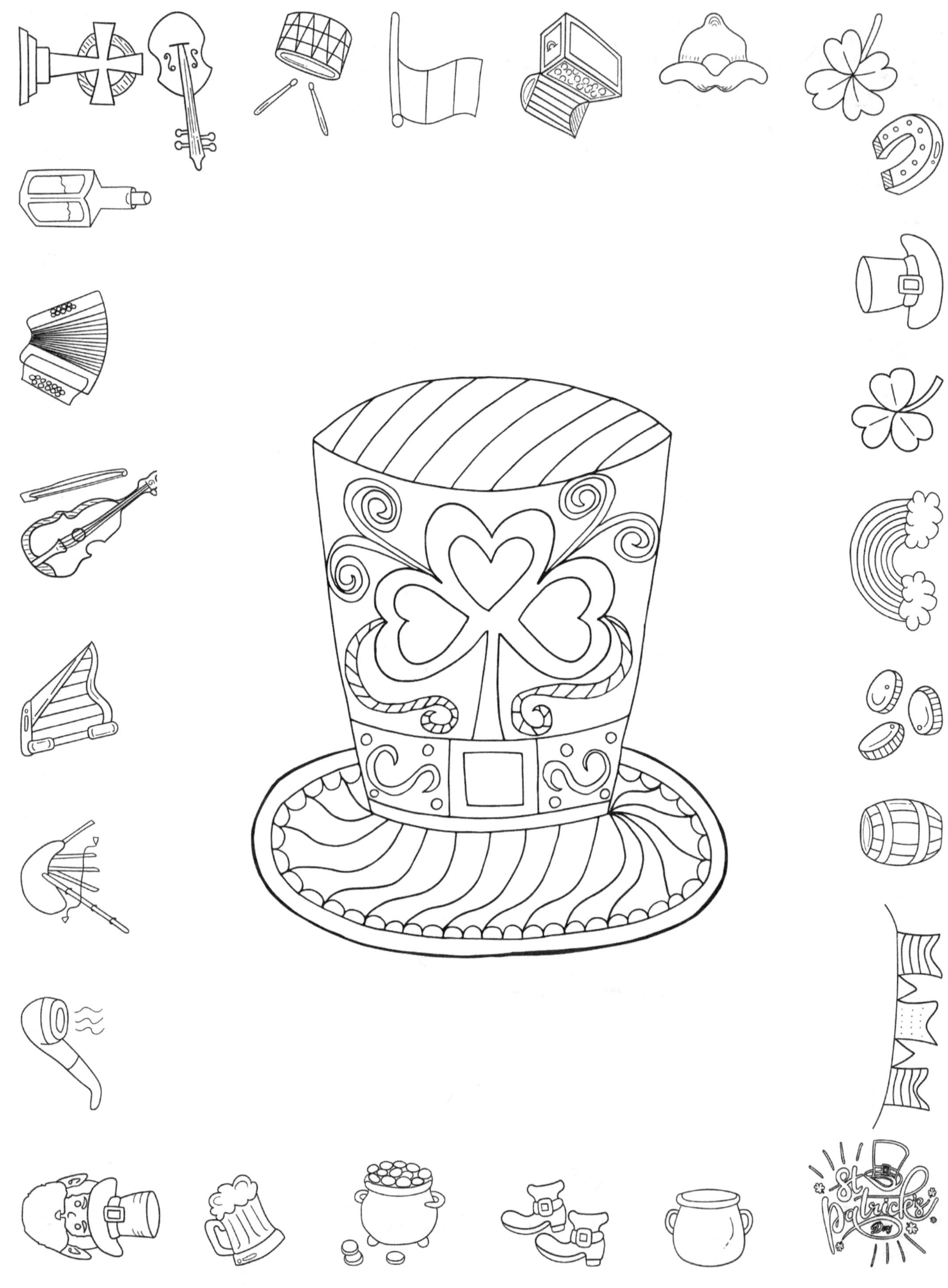

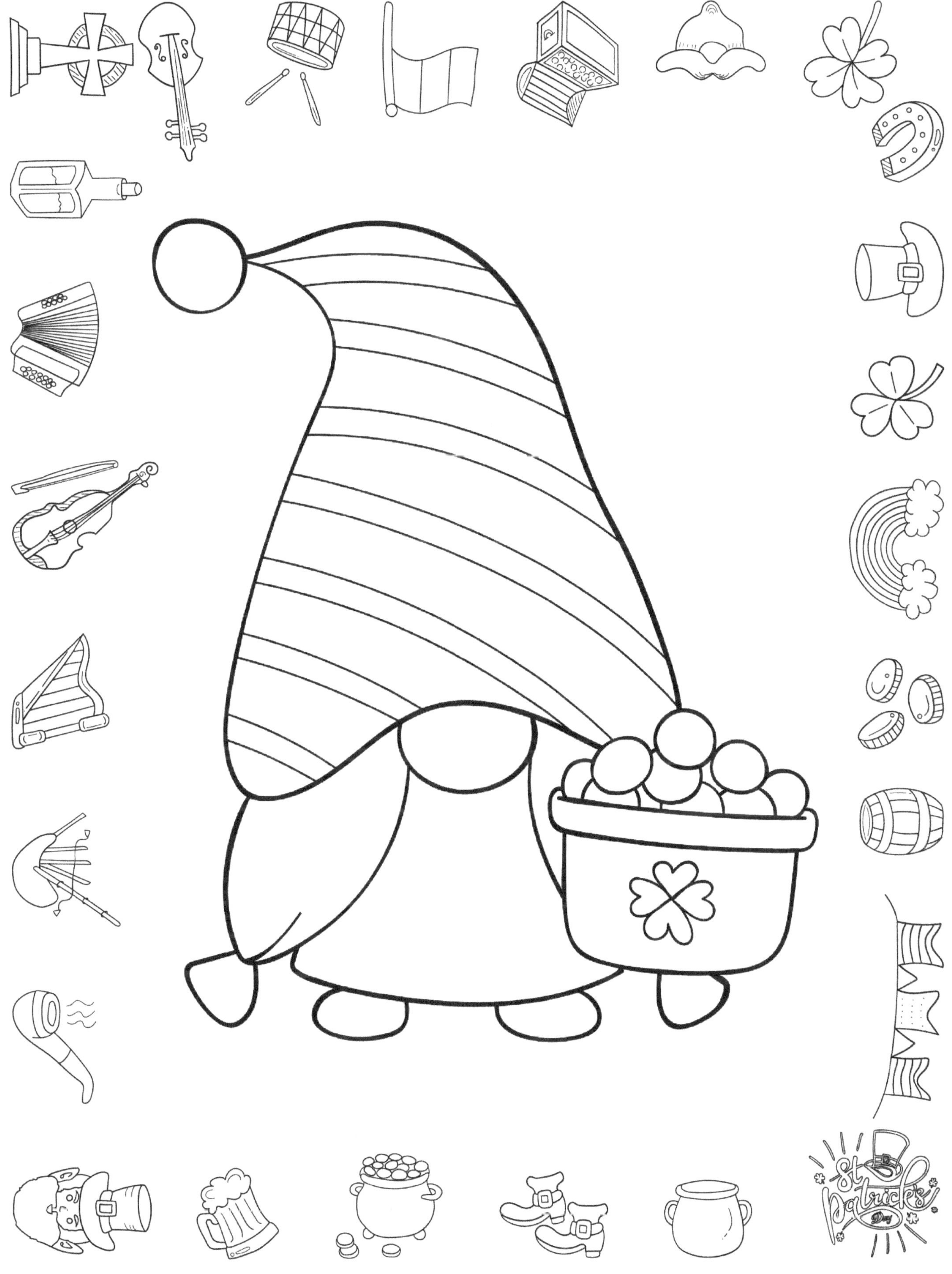

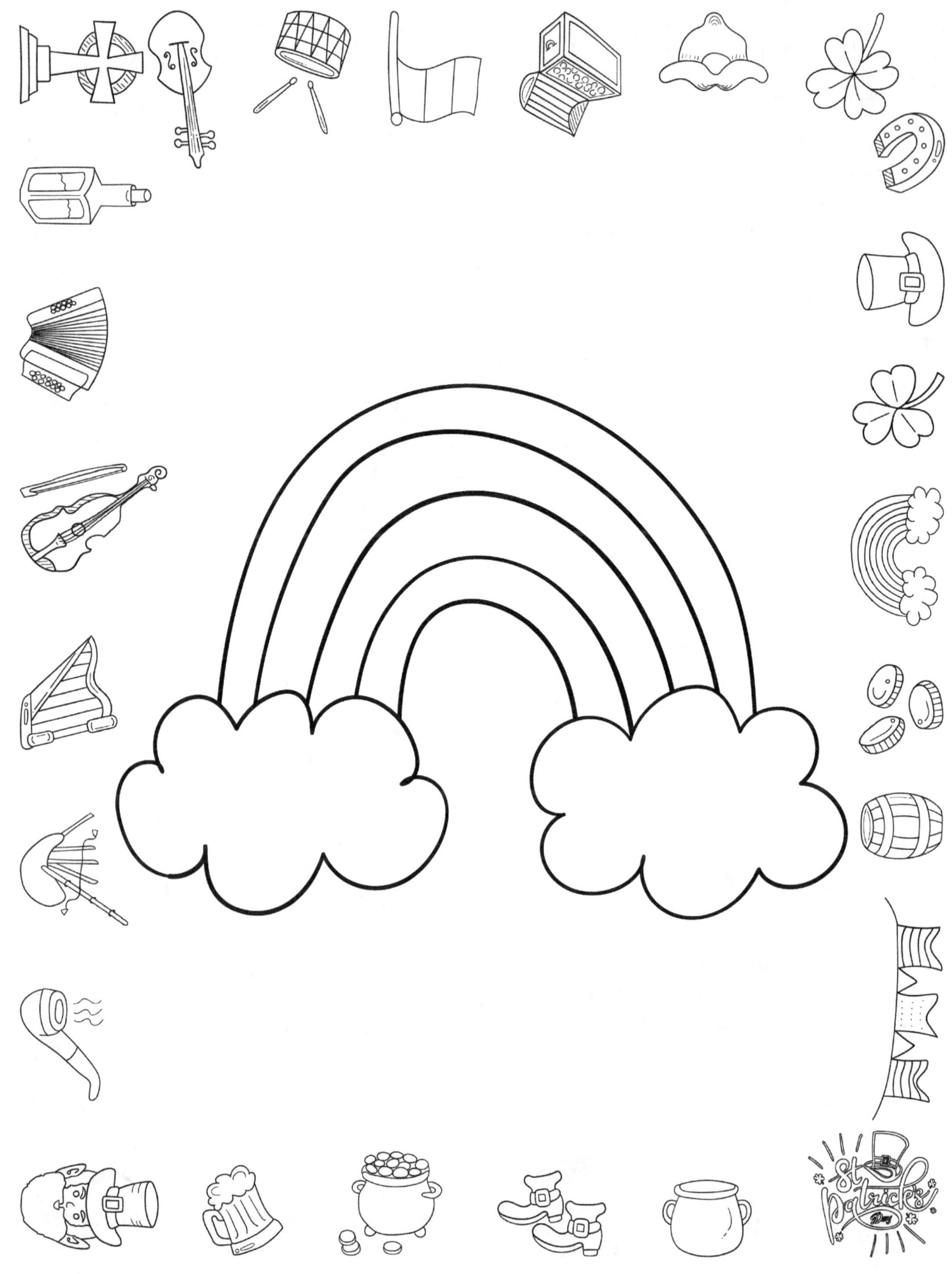

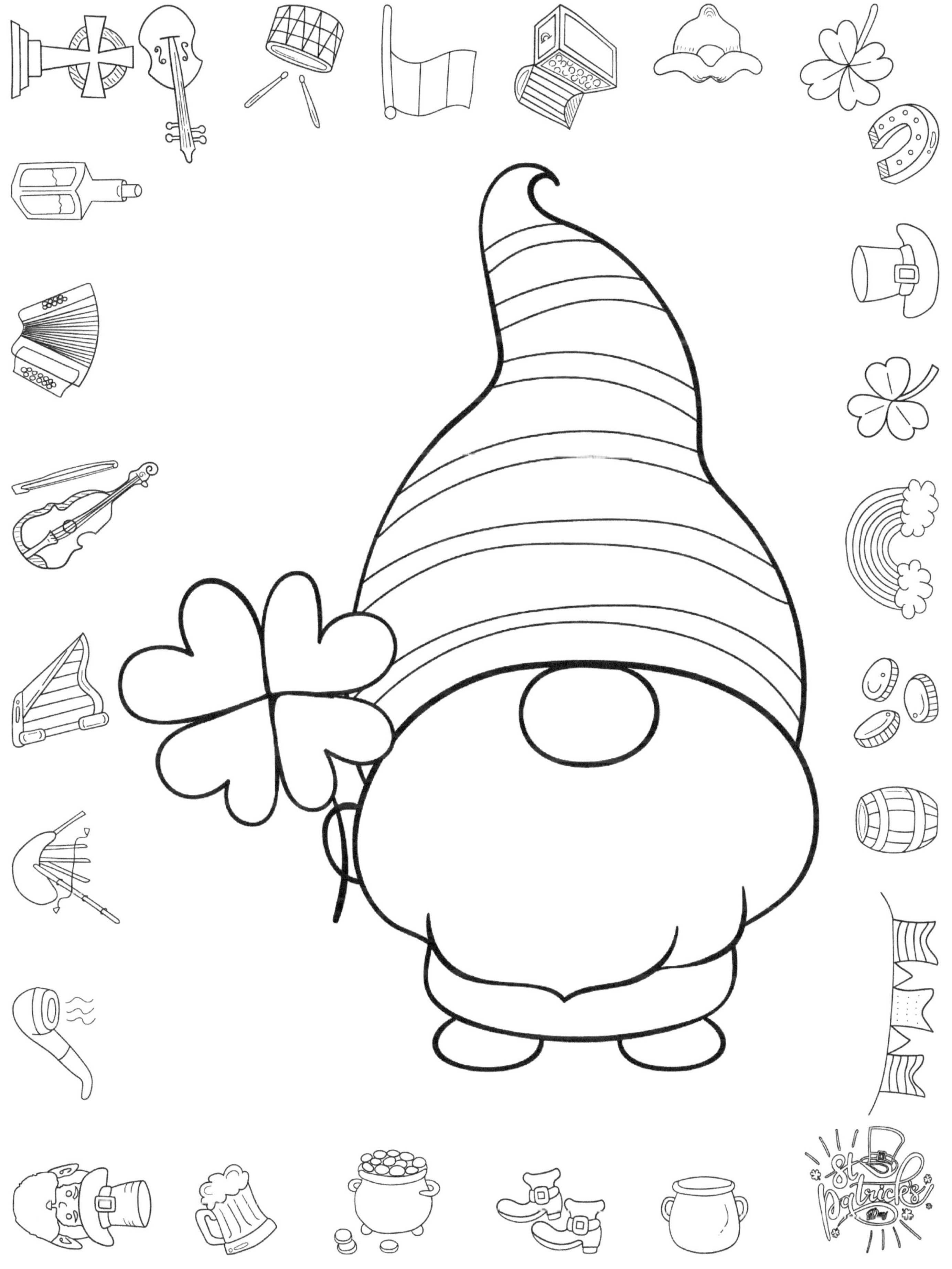

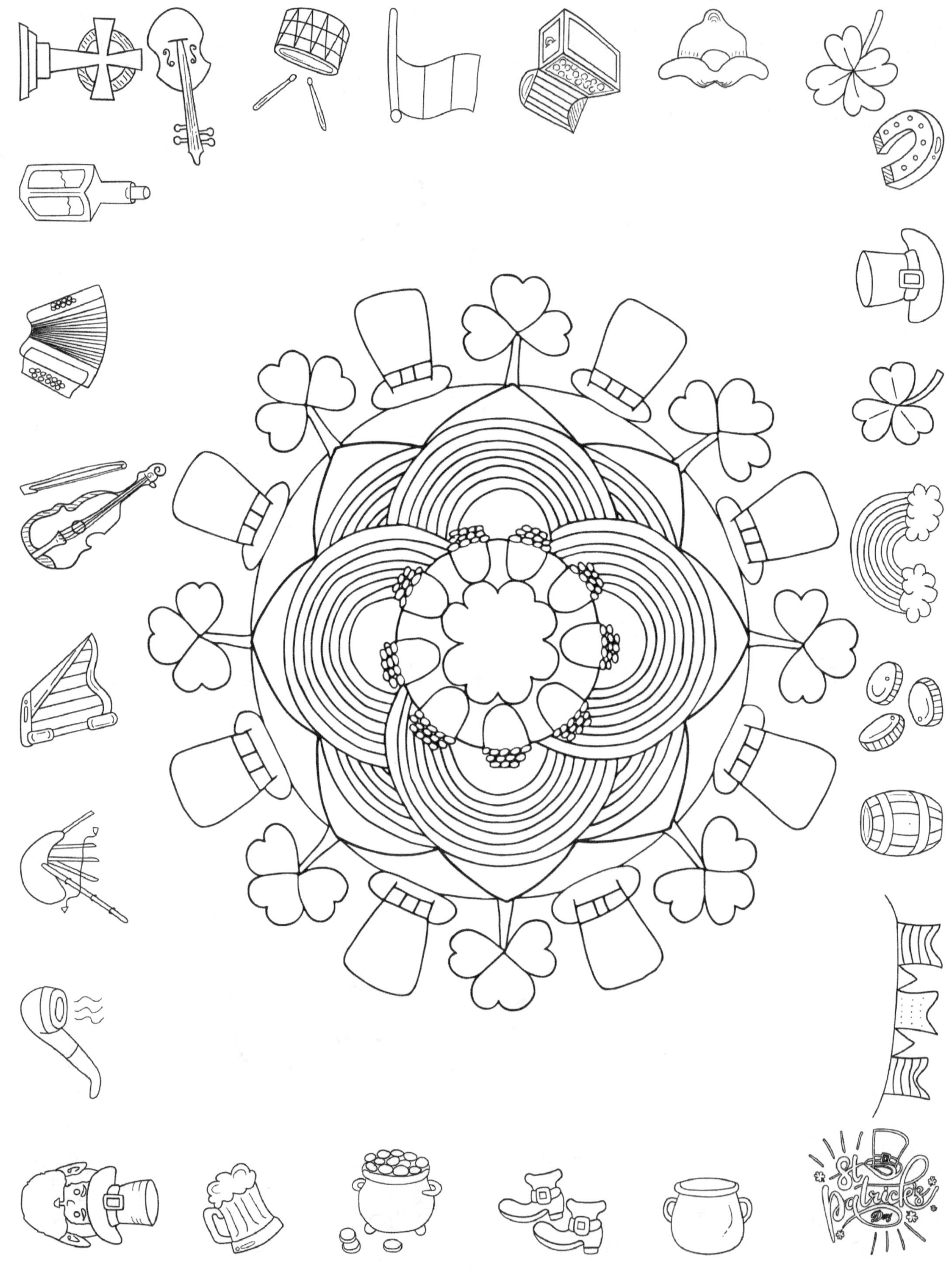

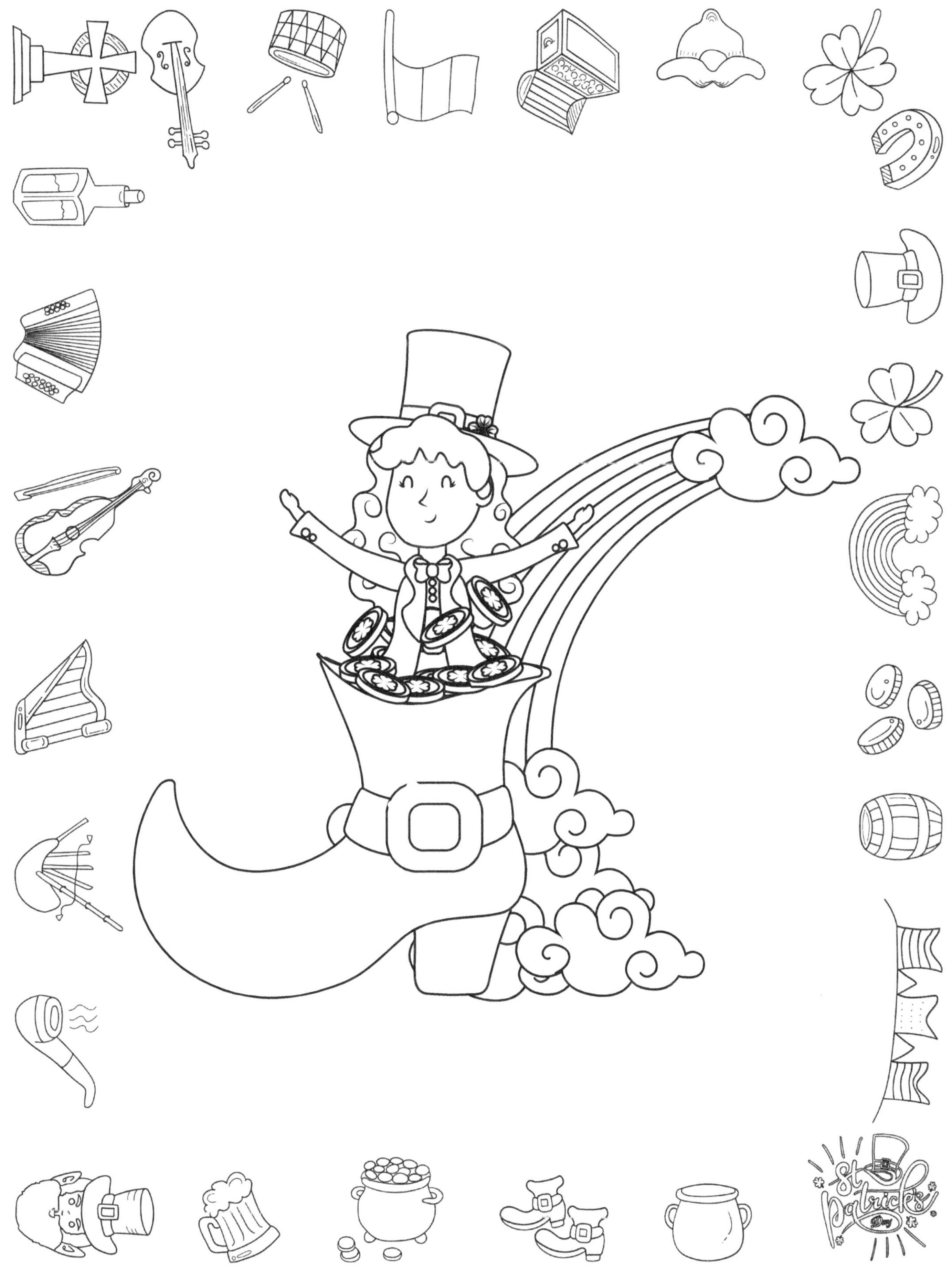

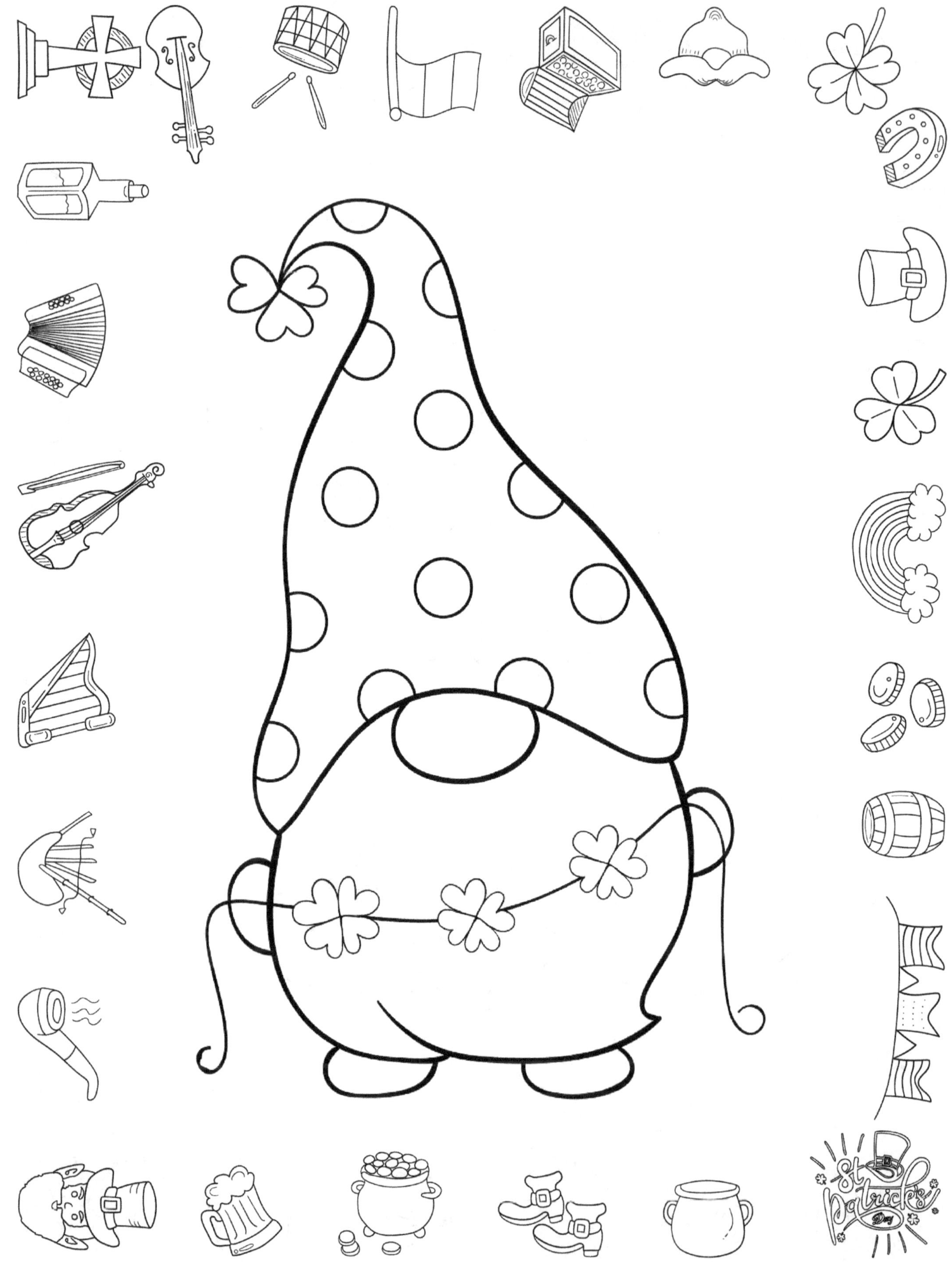

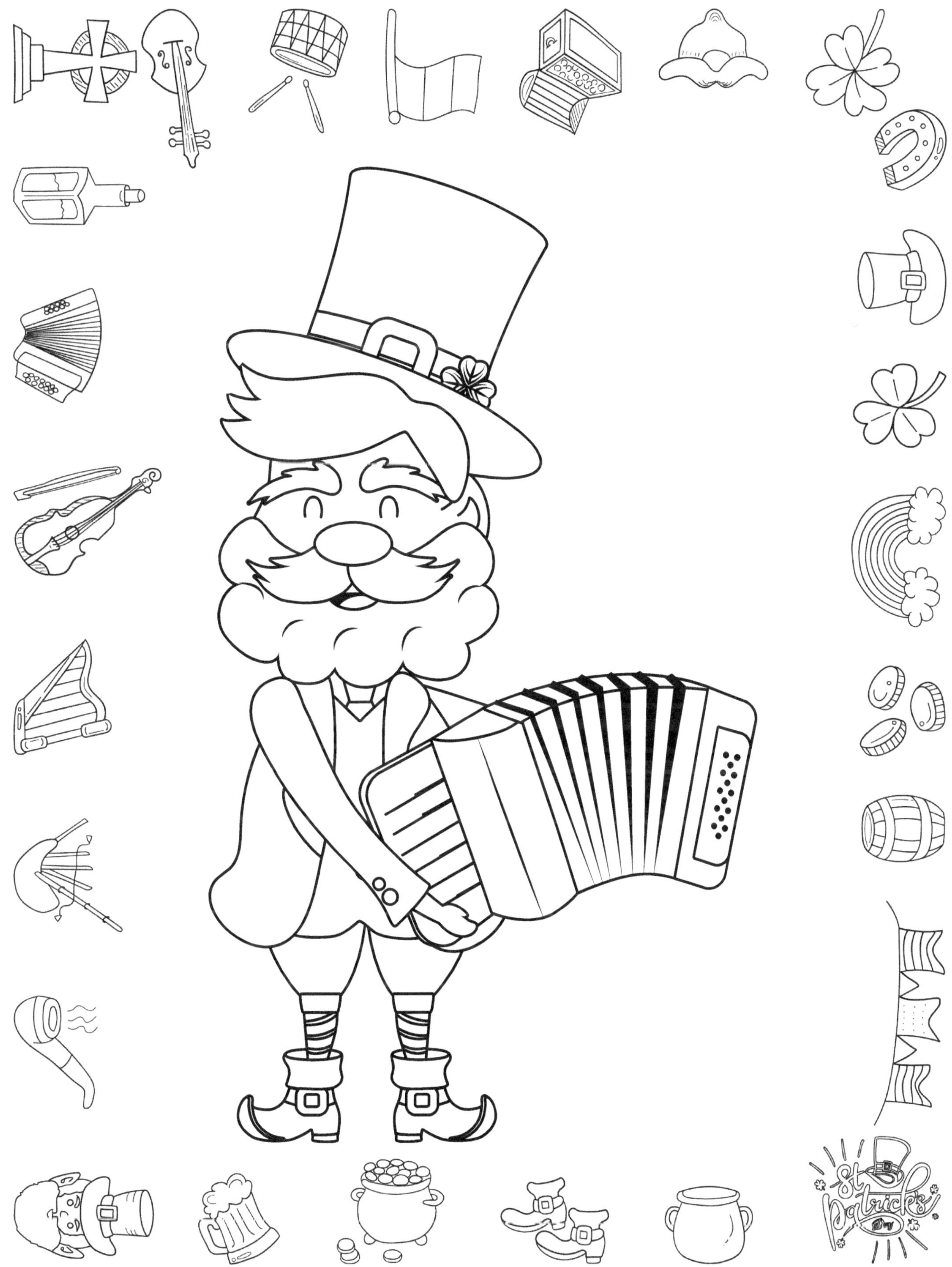

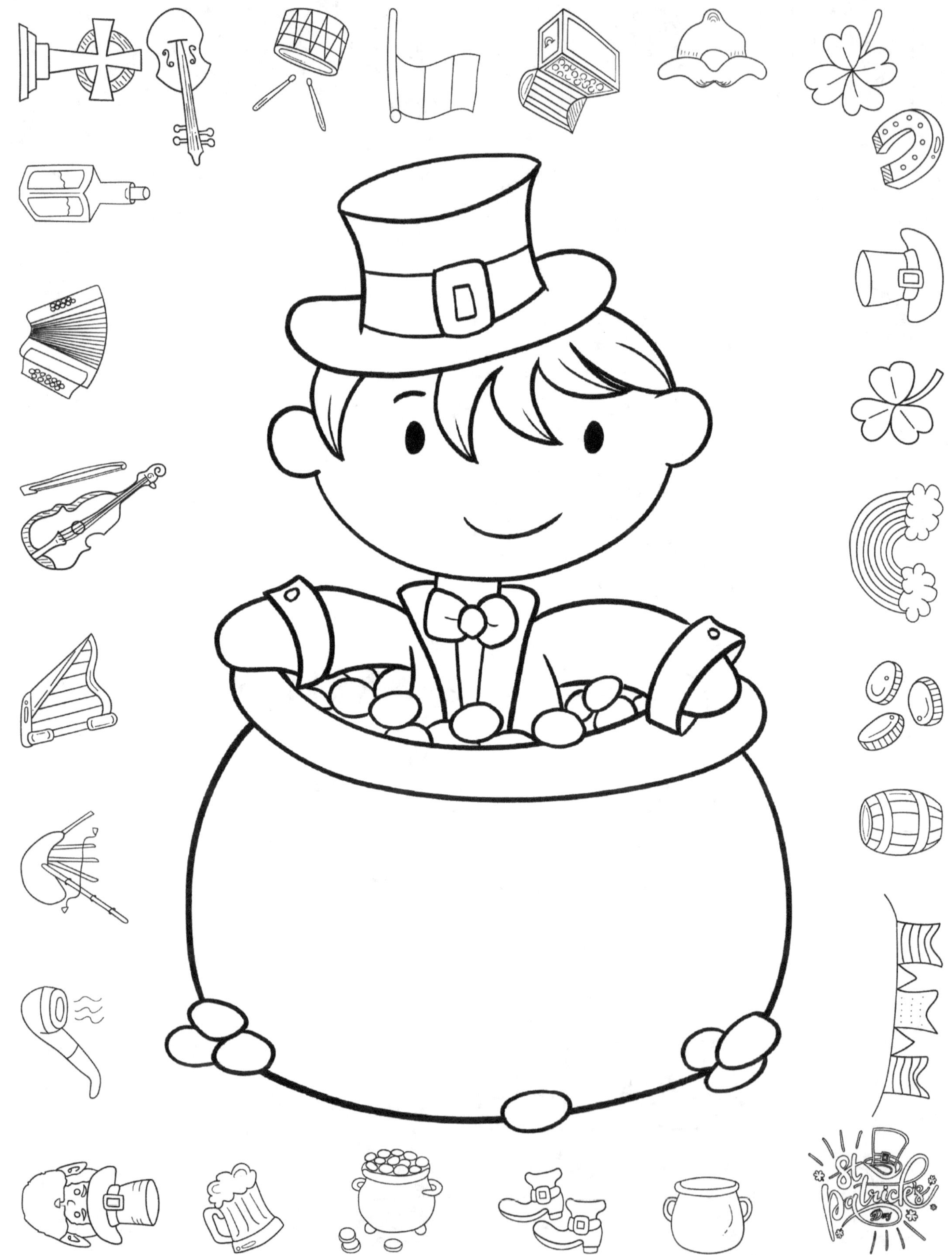

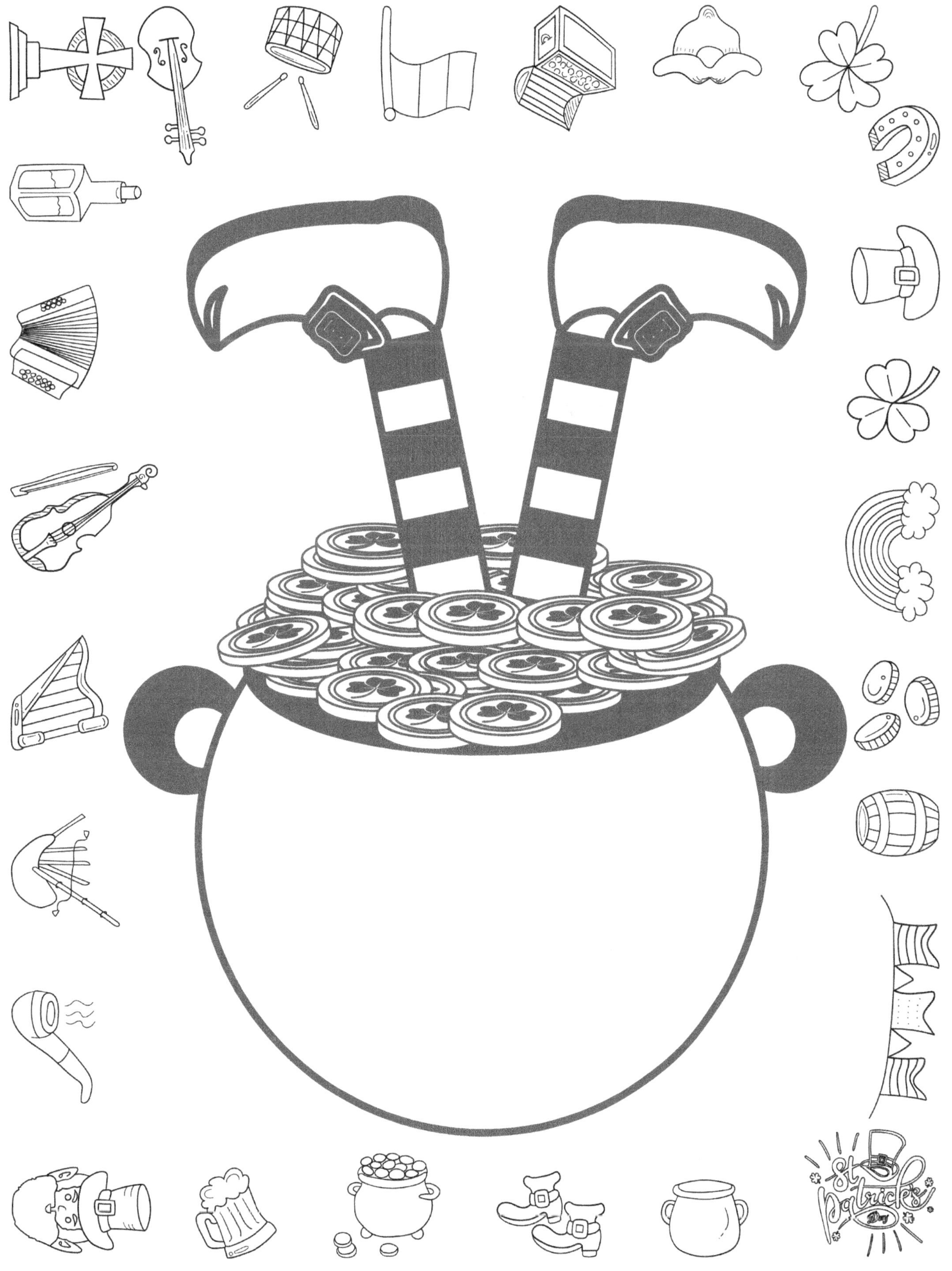

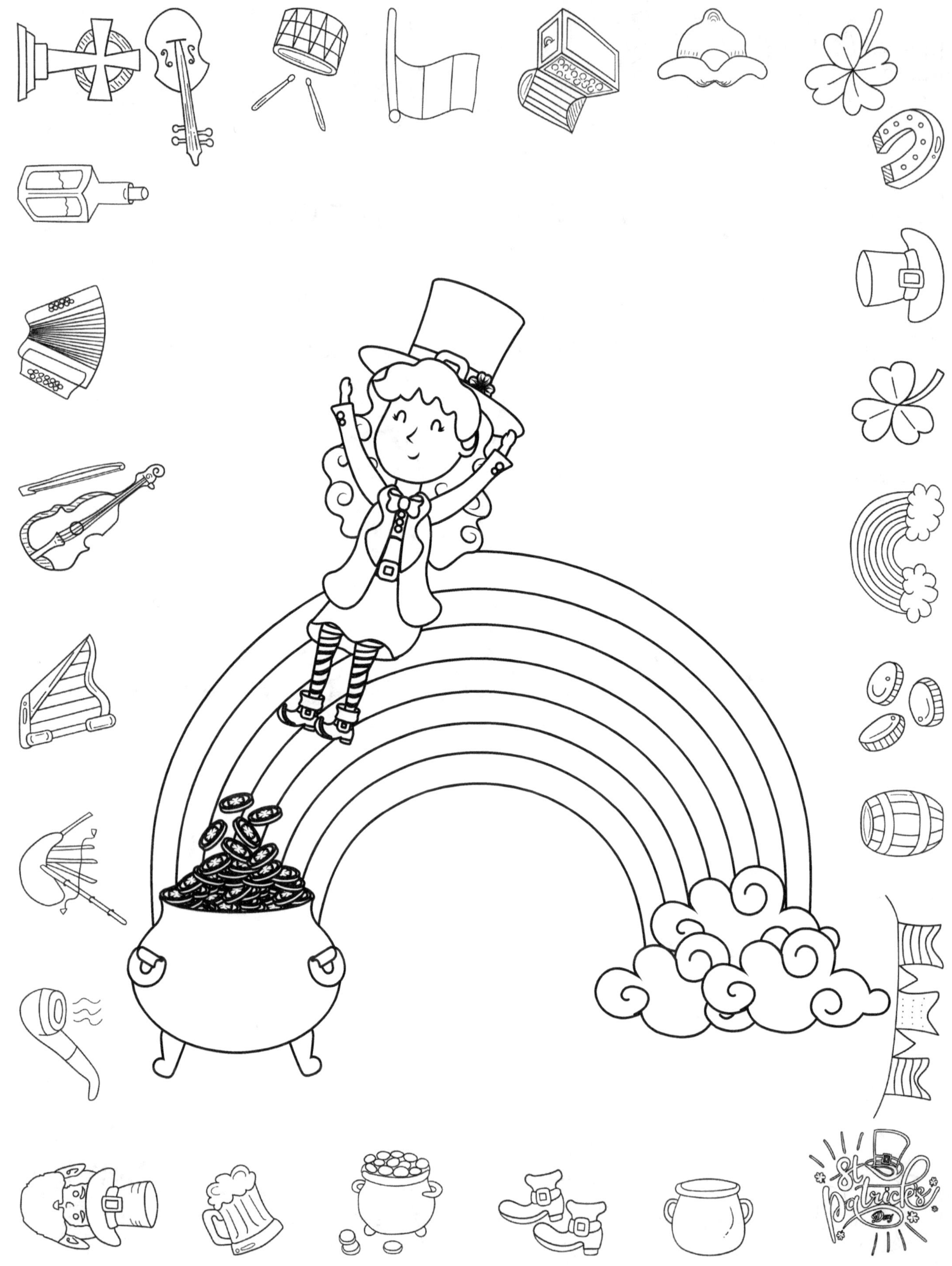

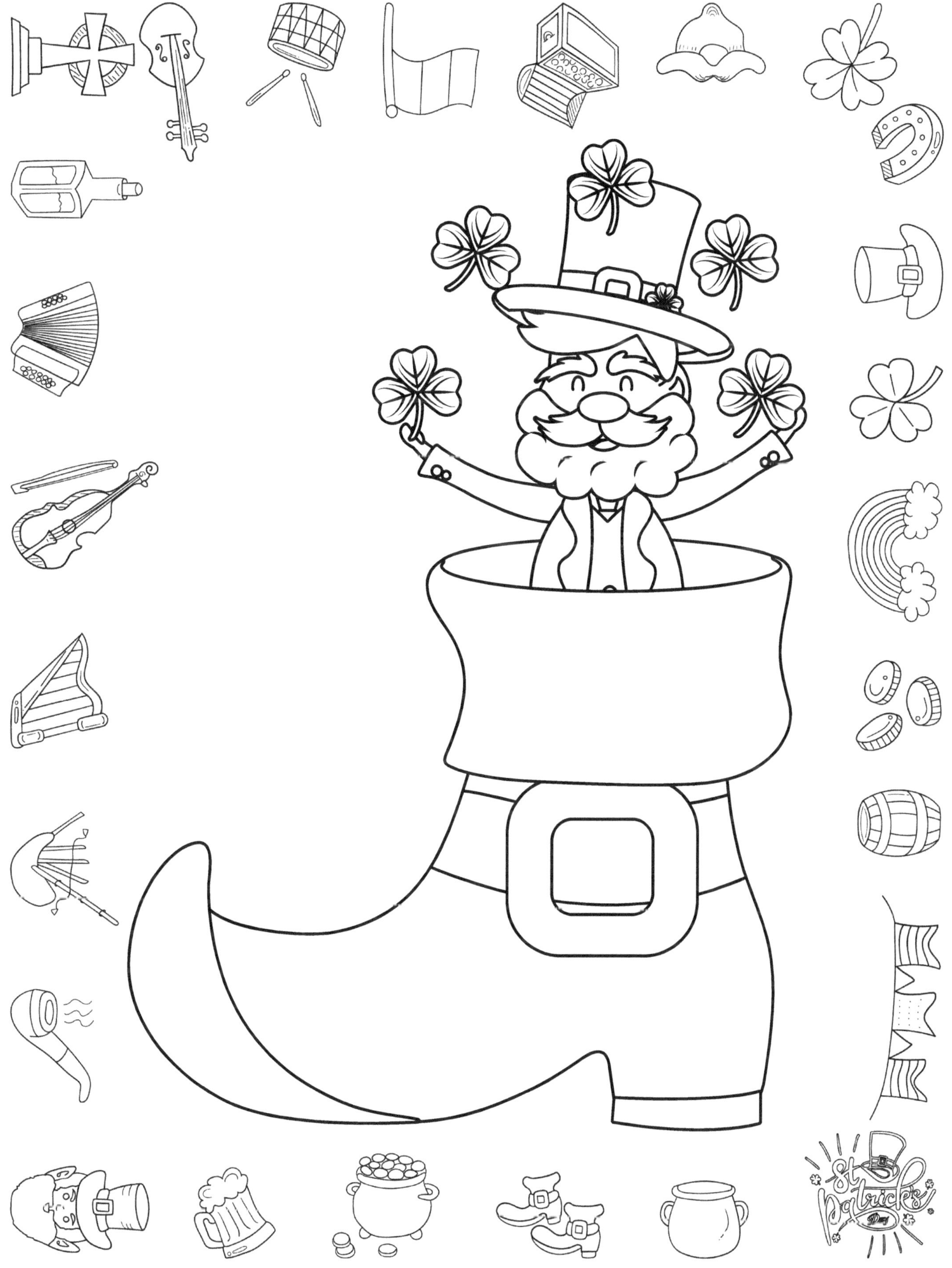

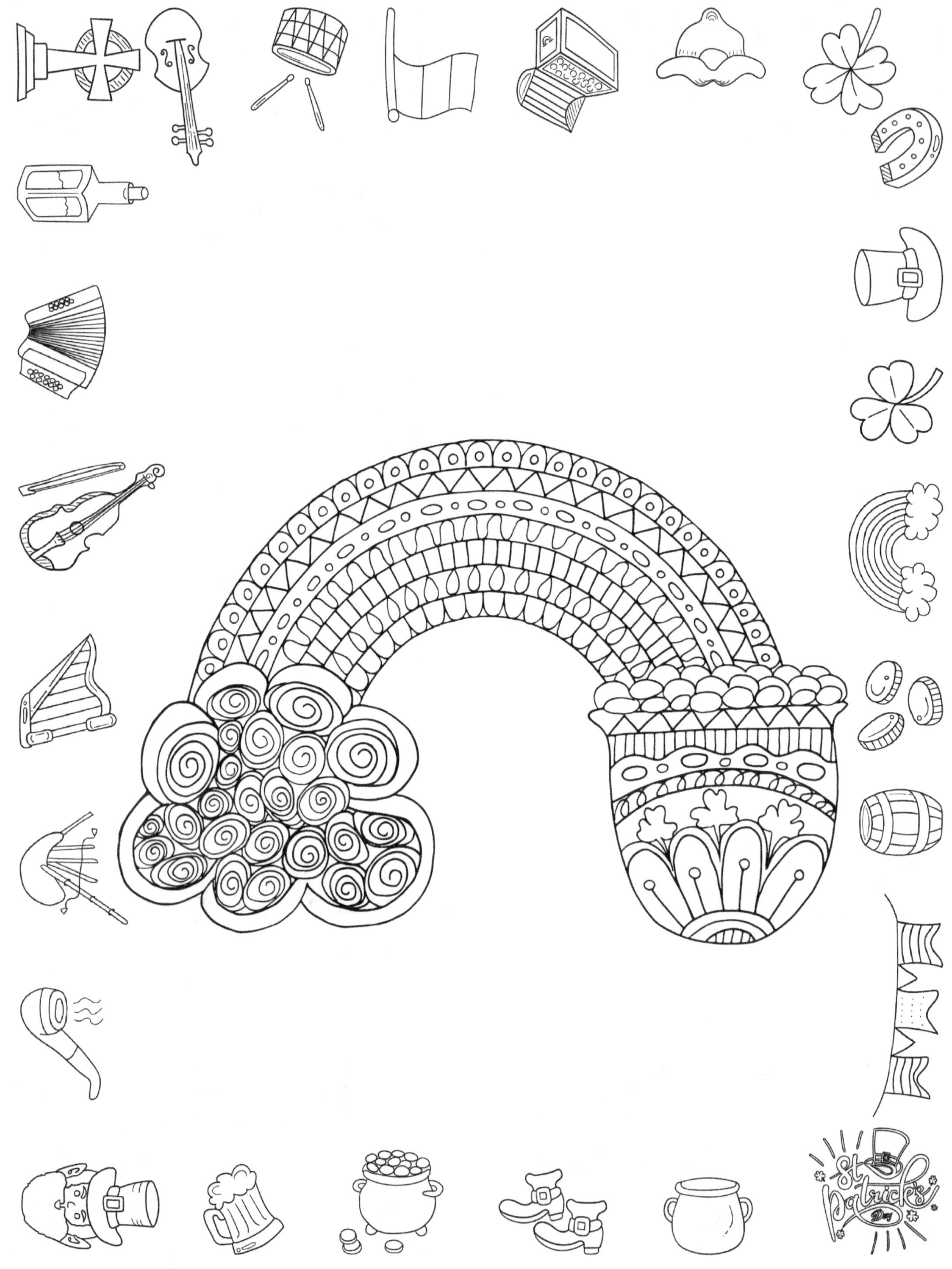

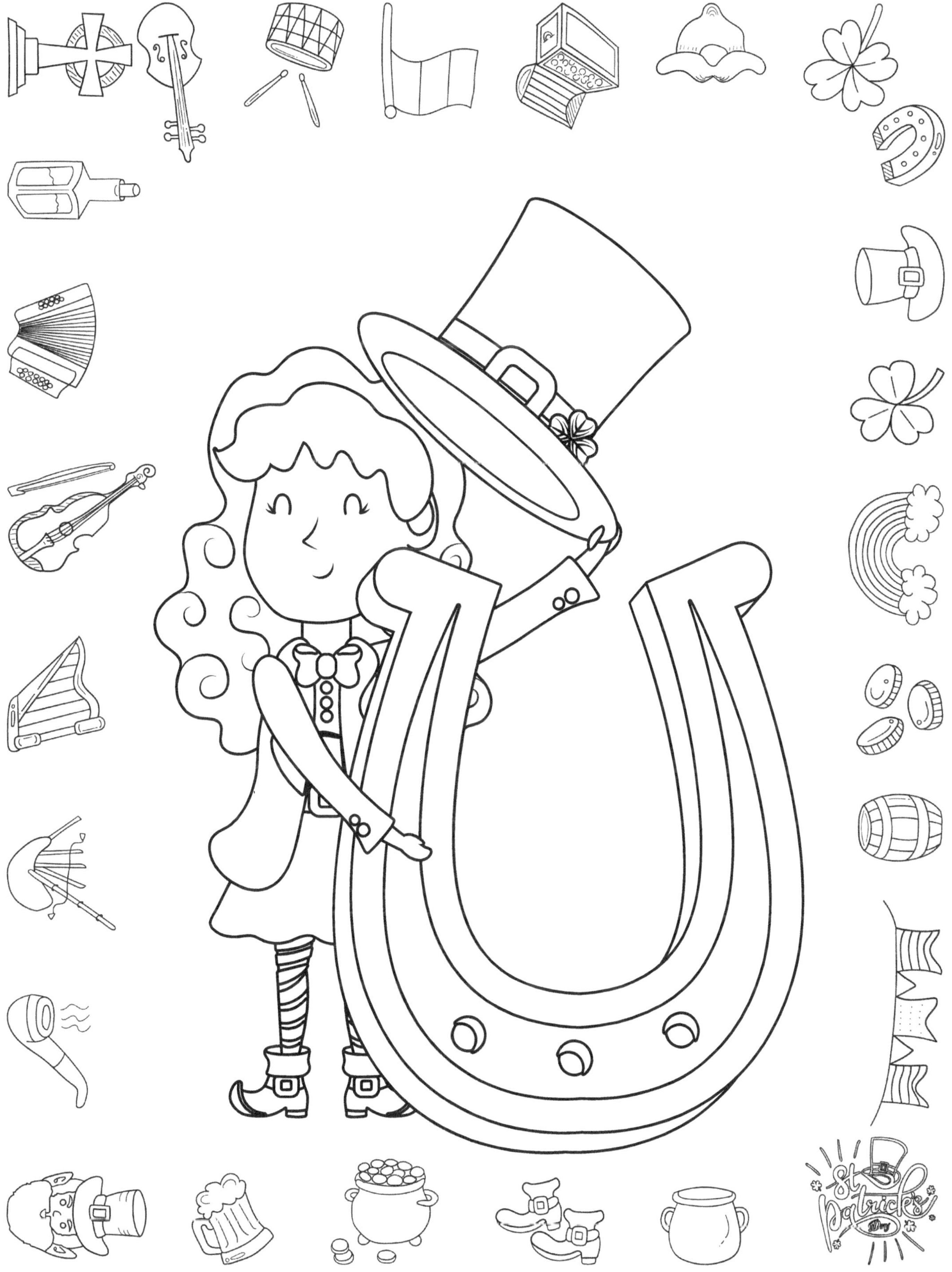

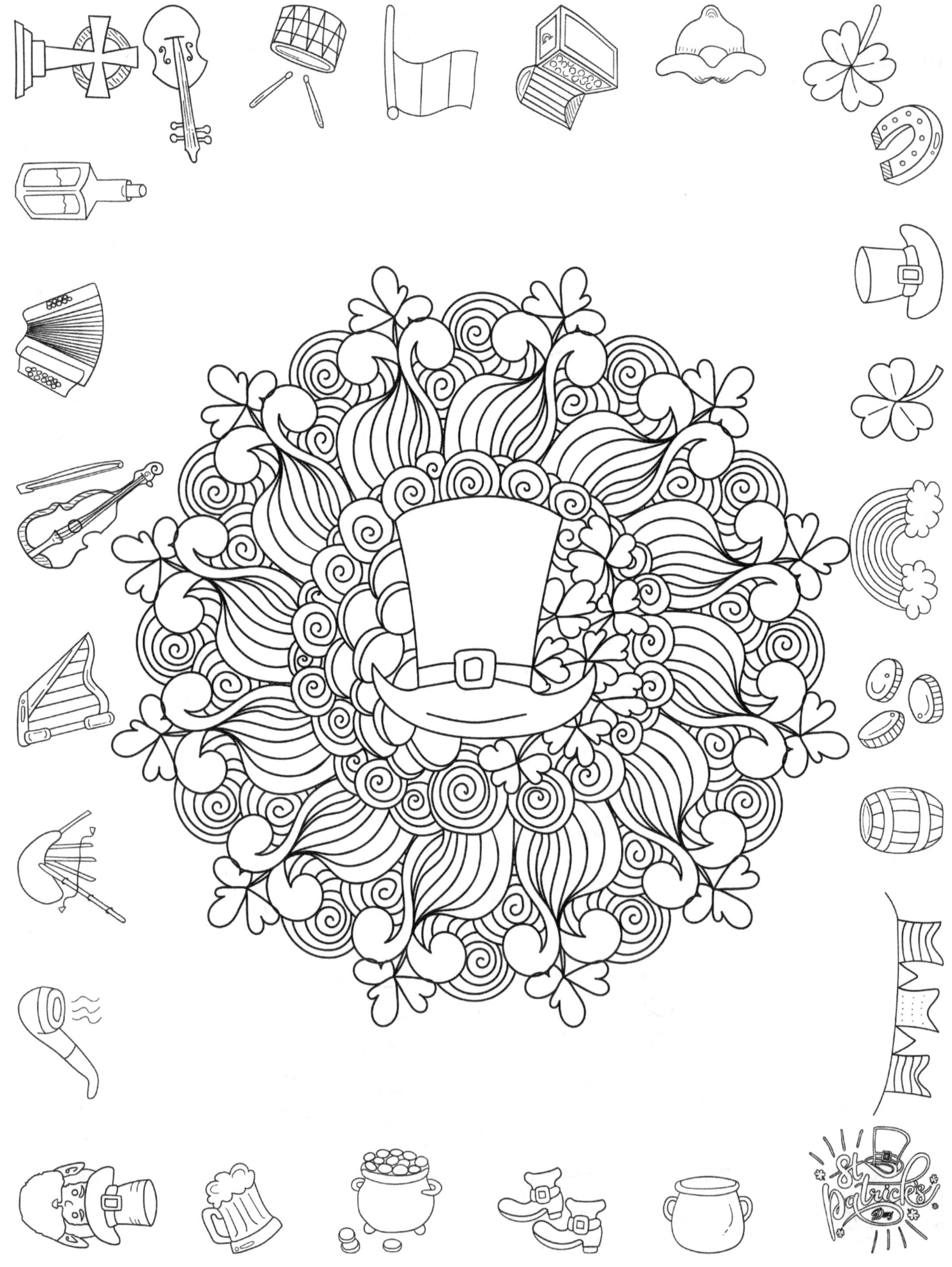

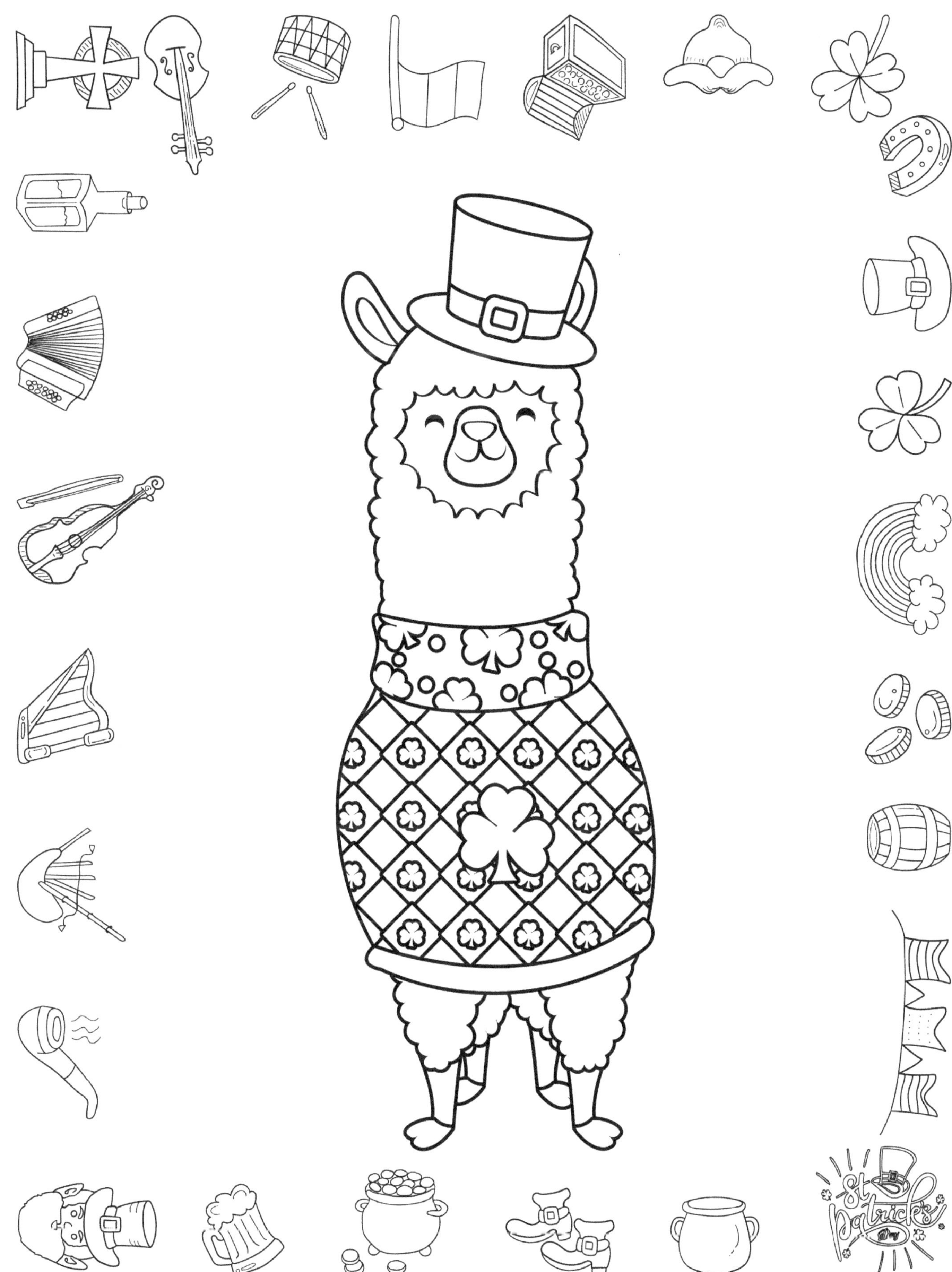

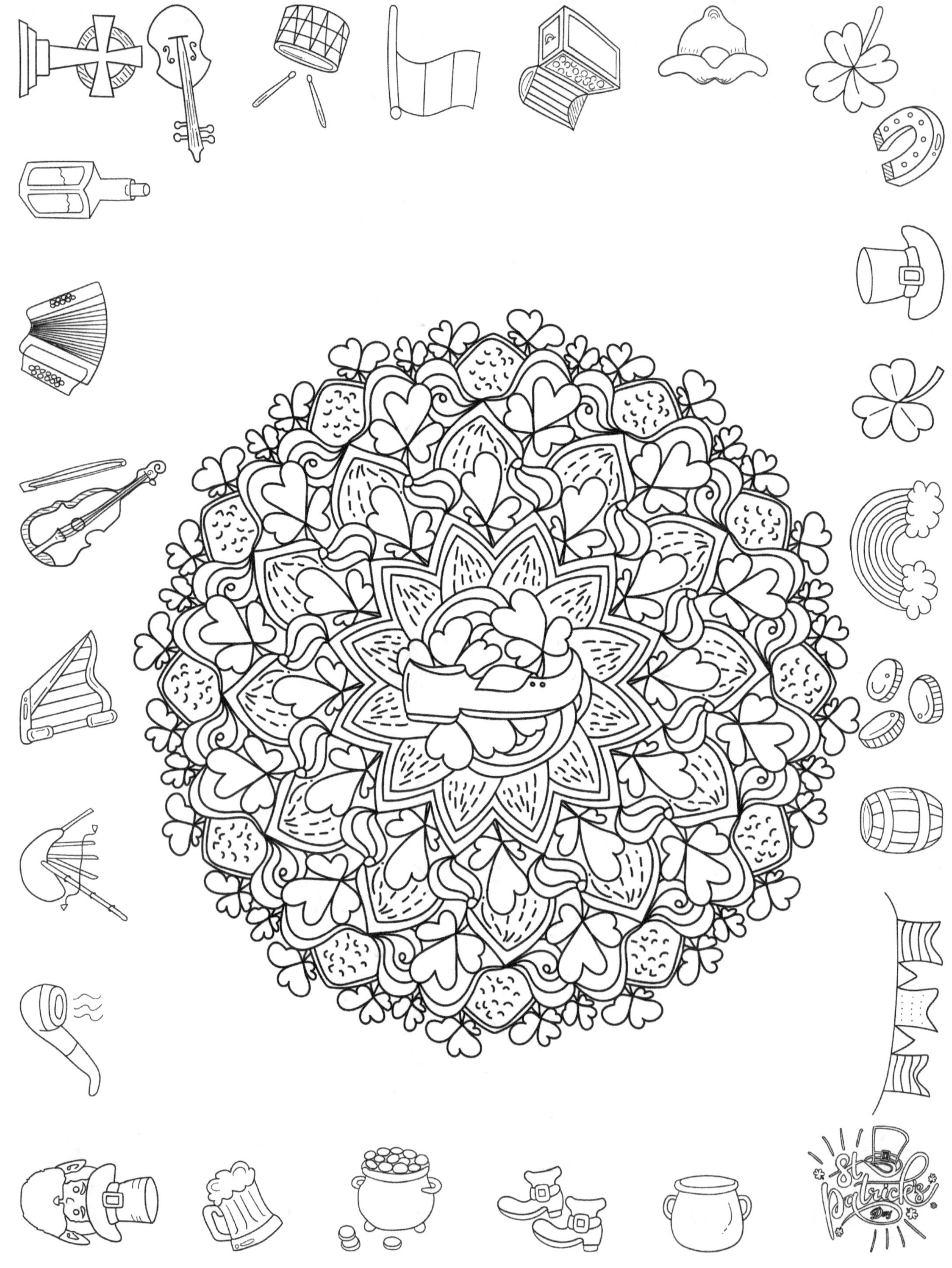

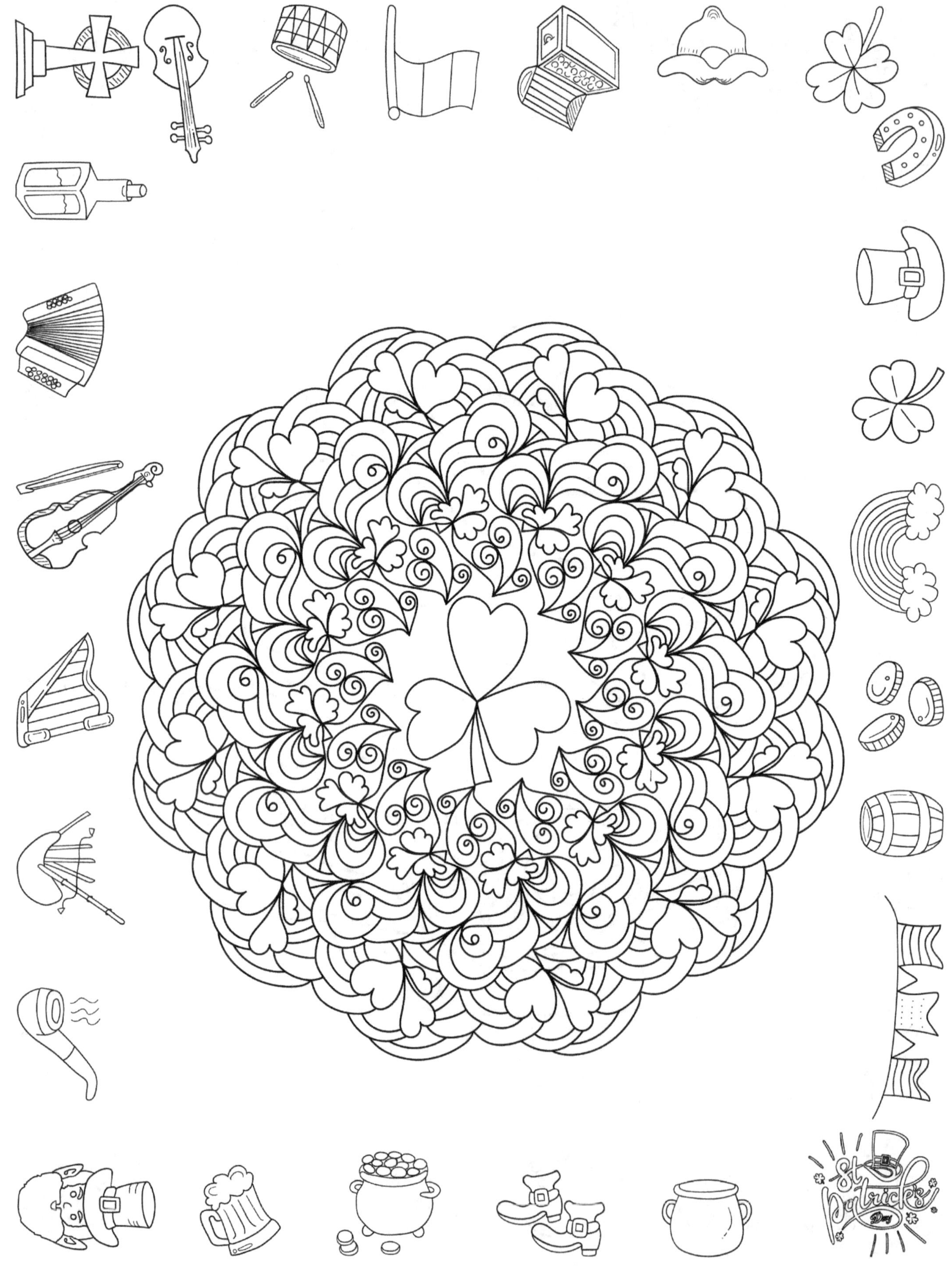

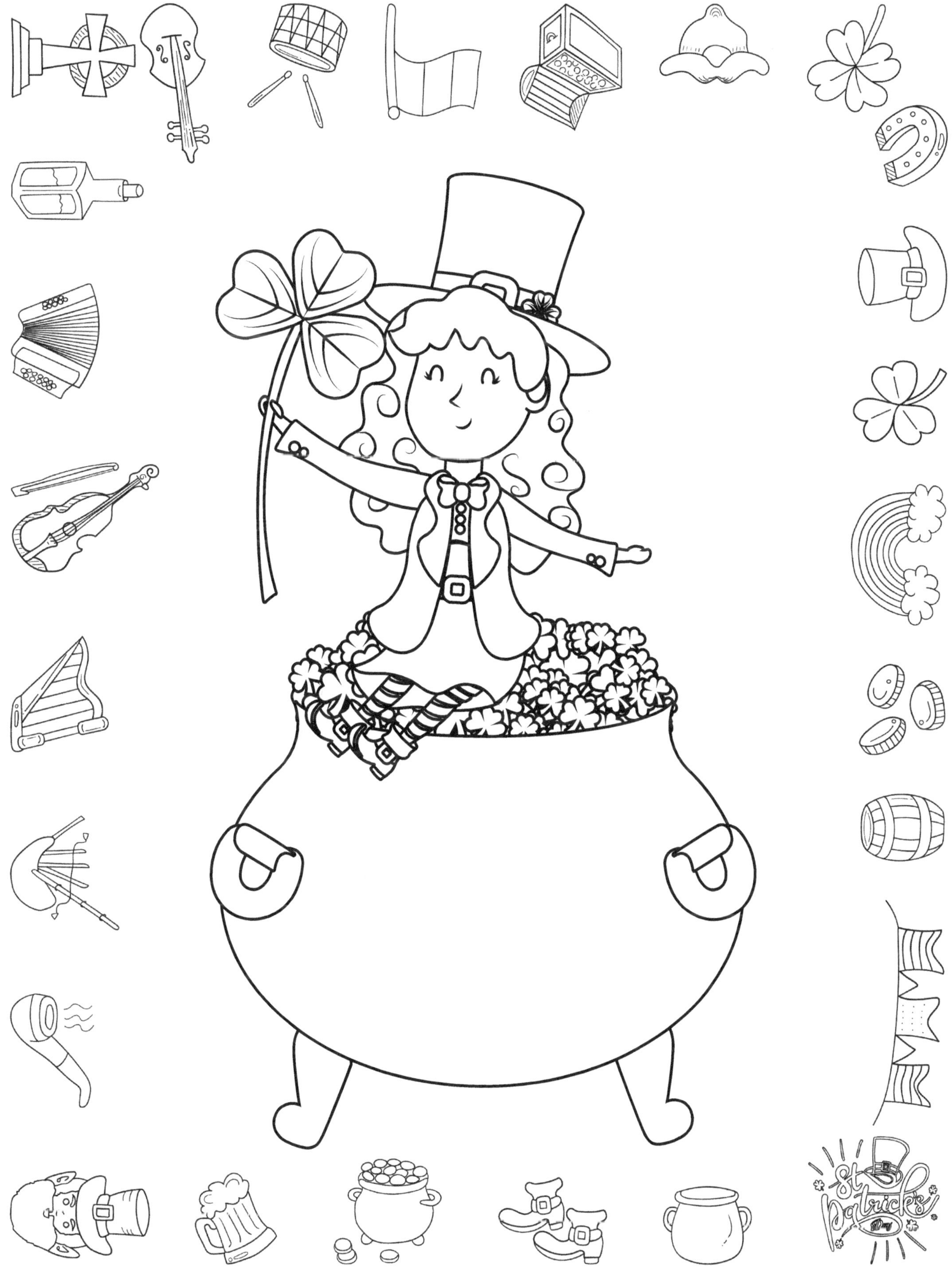

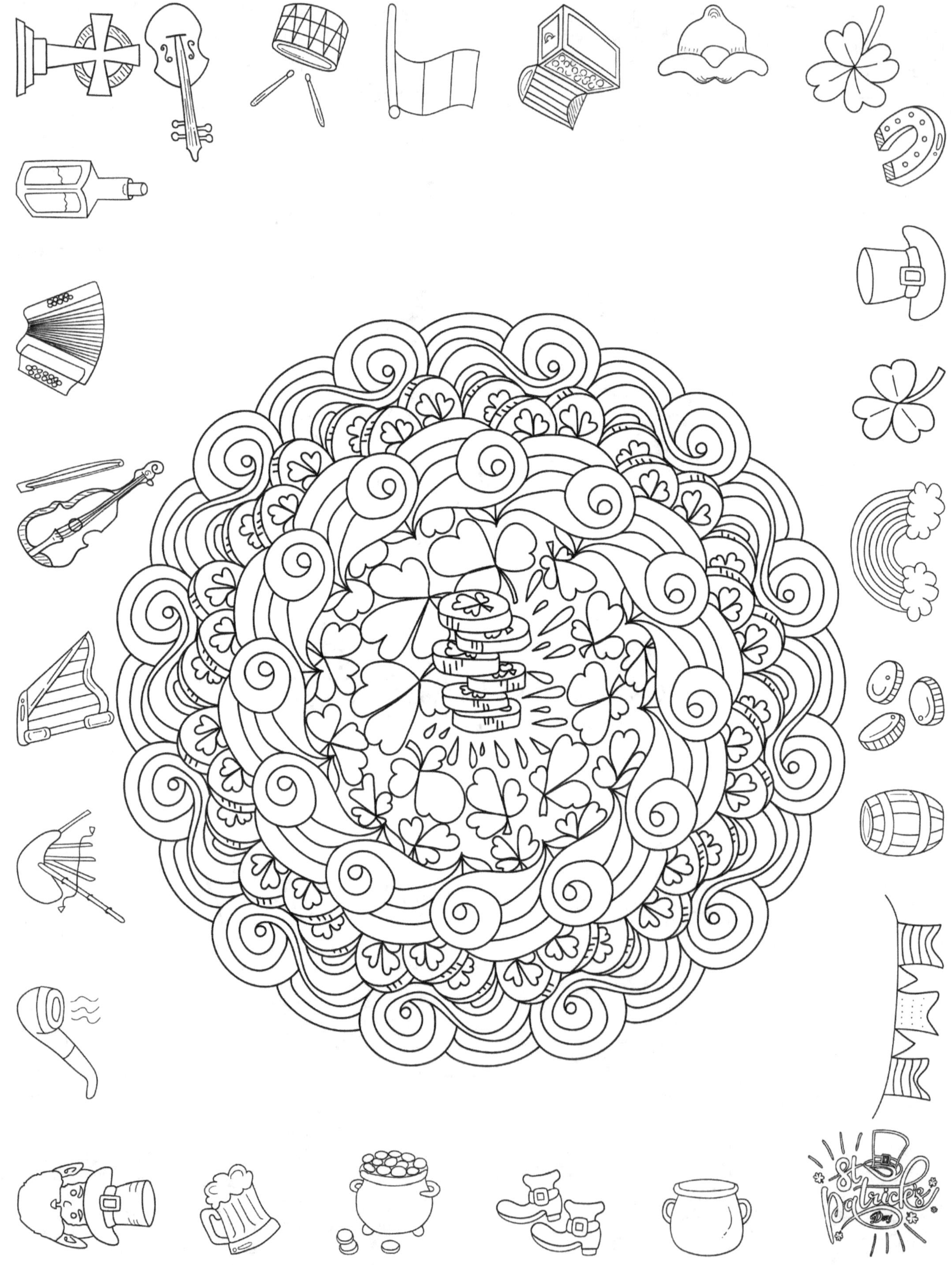

St Patrick's Day

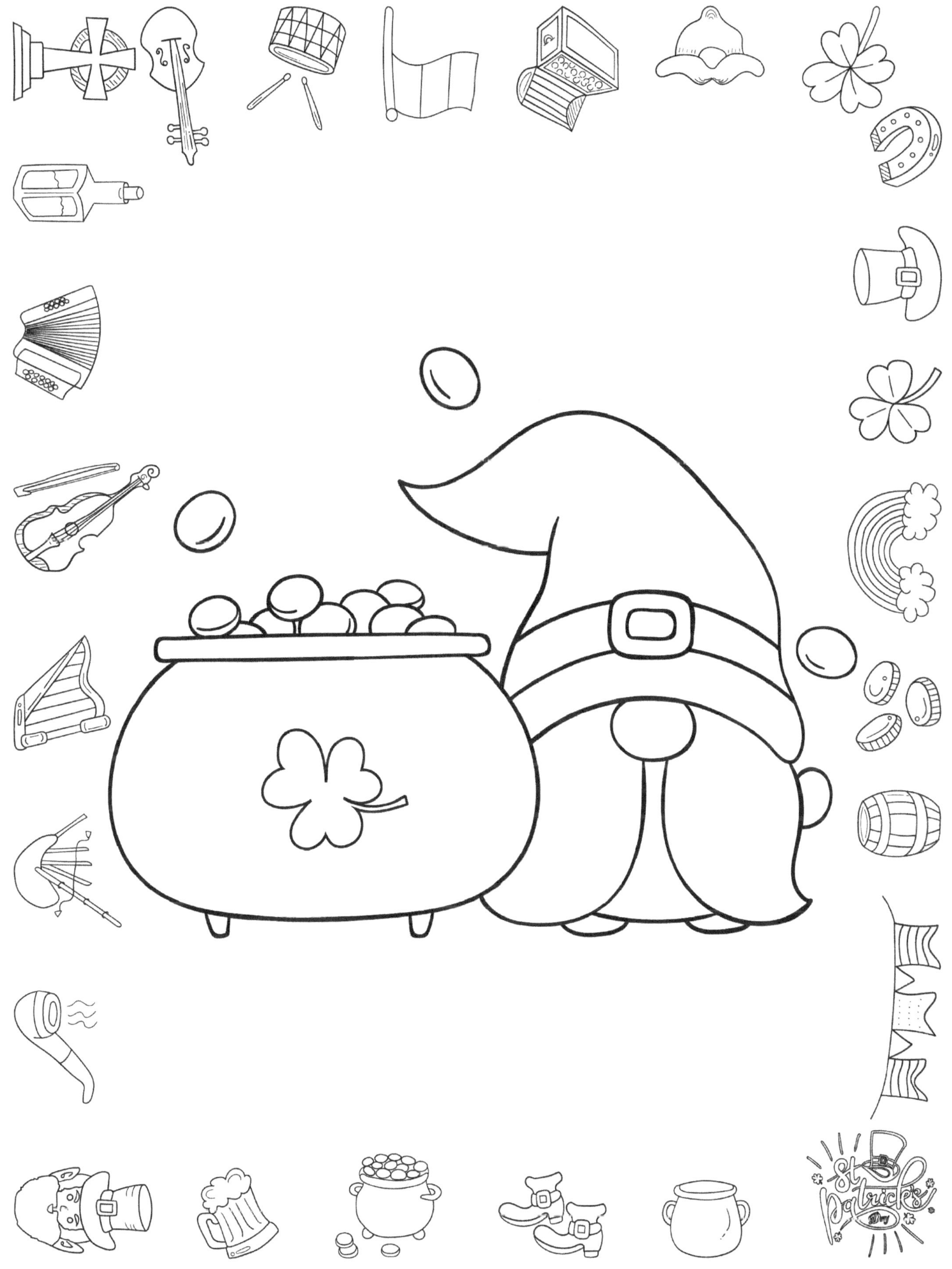

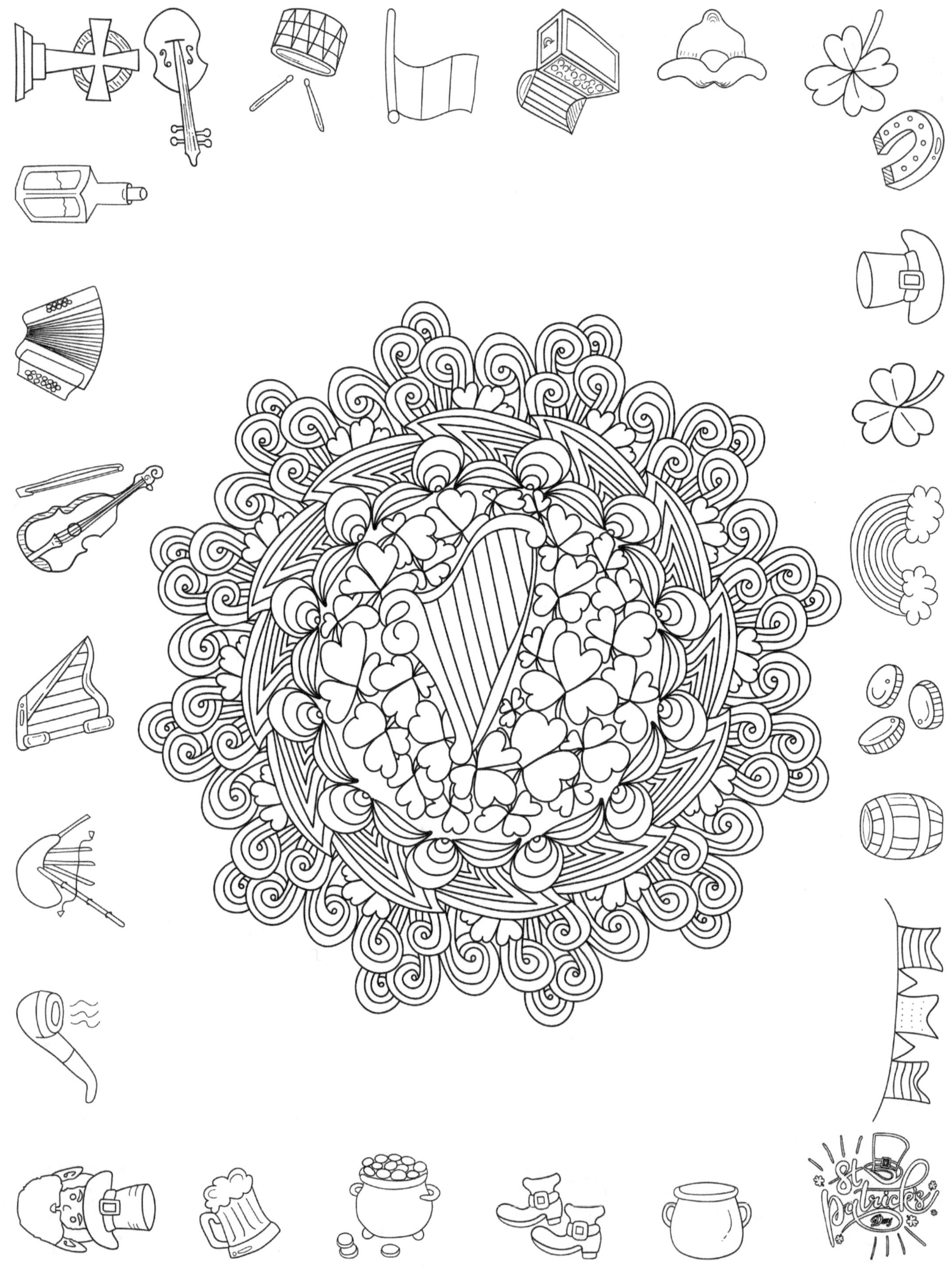

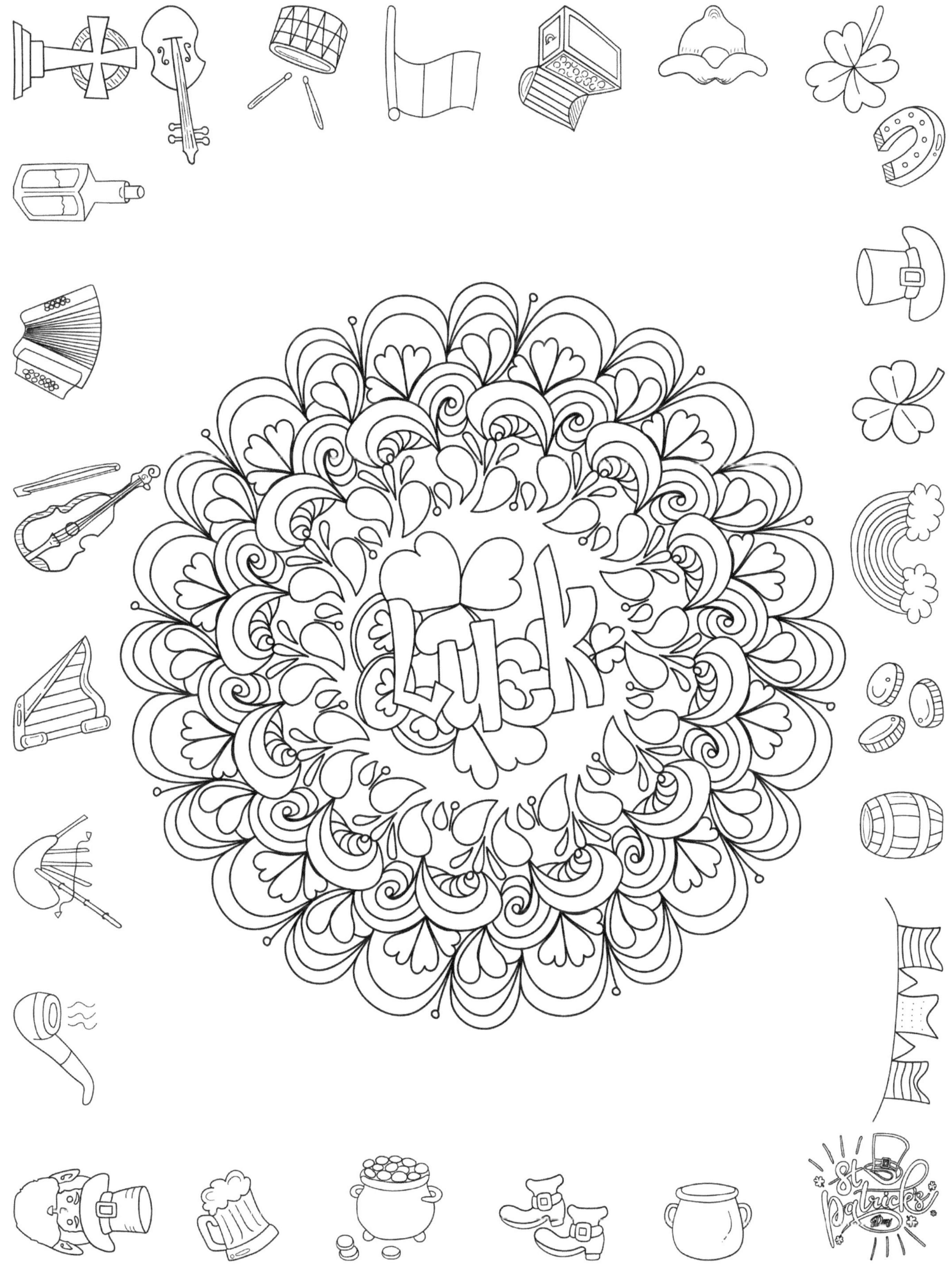

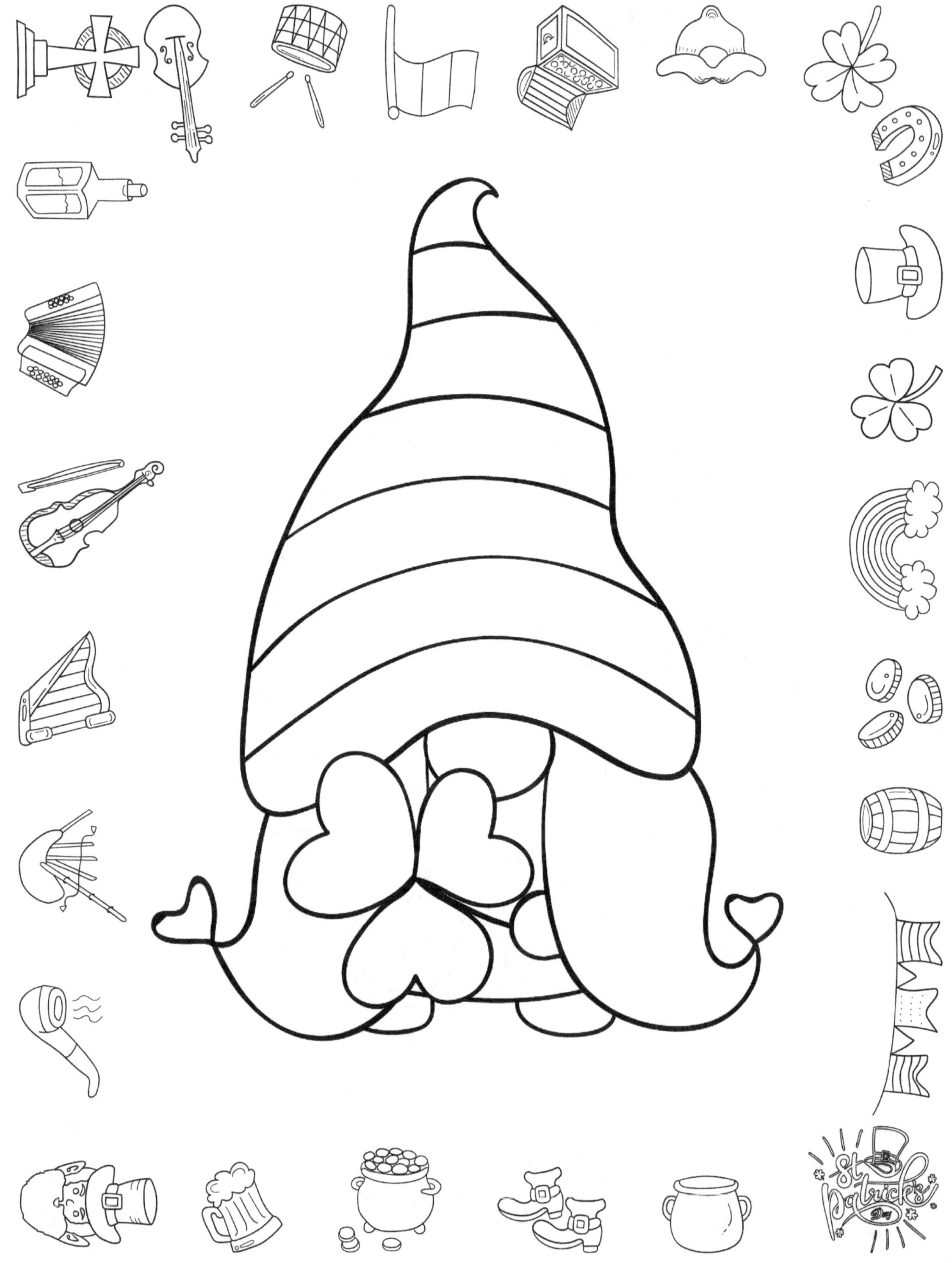

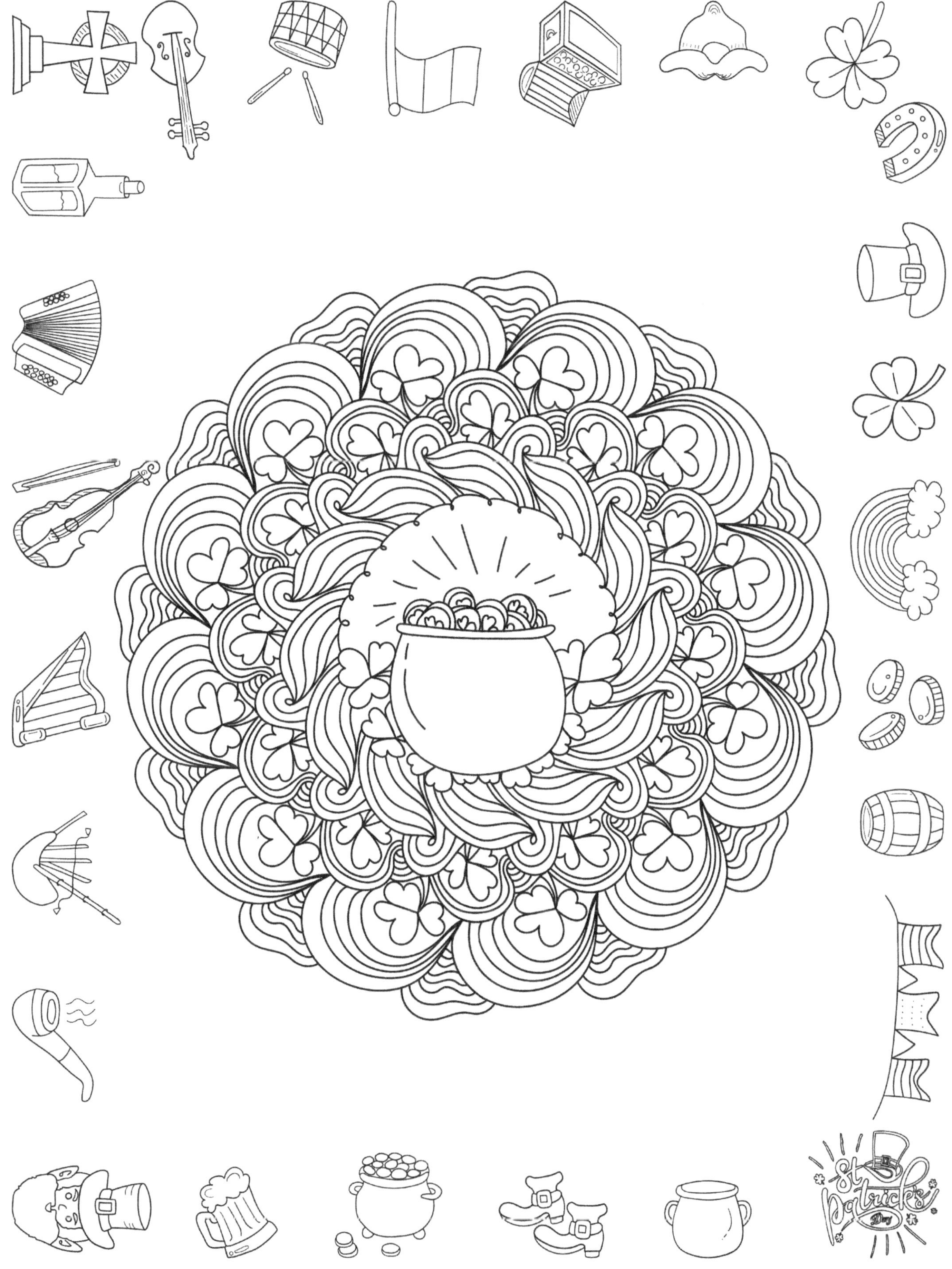
St Patrick's Day

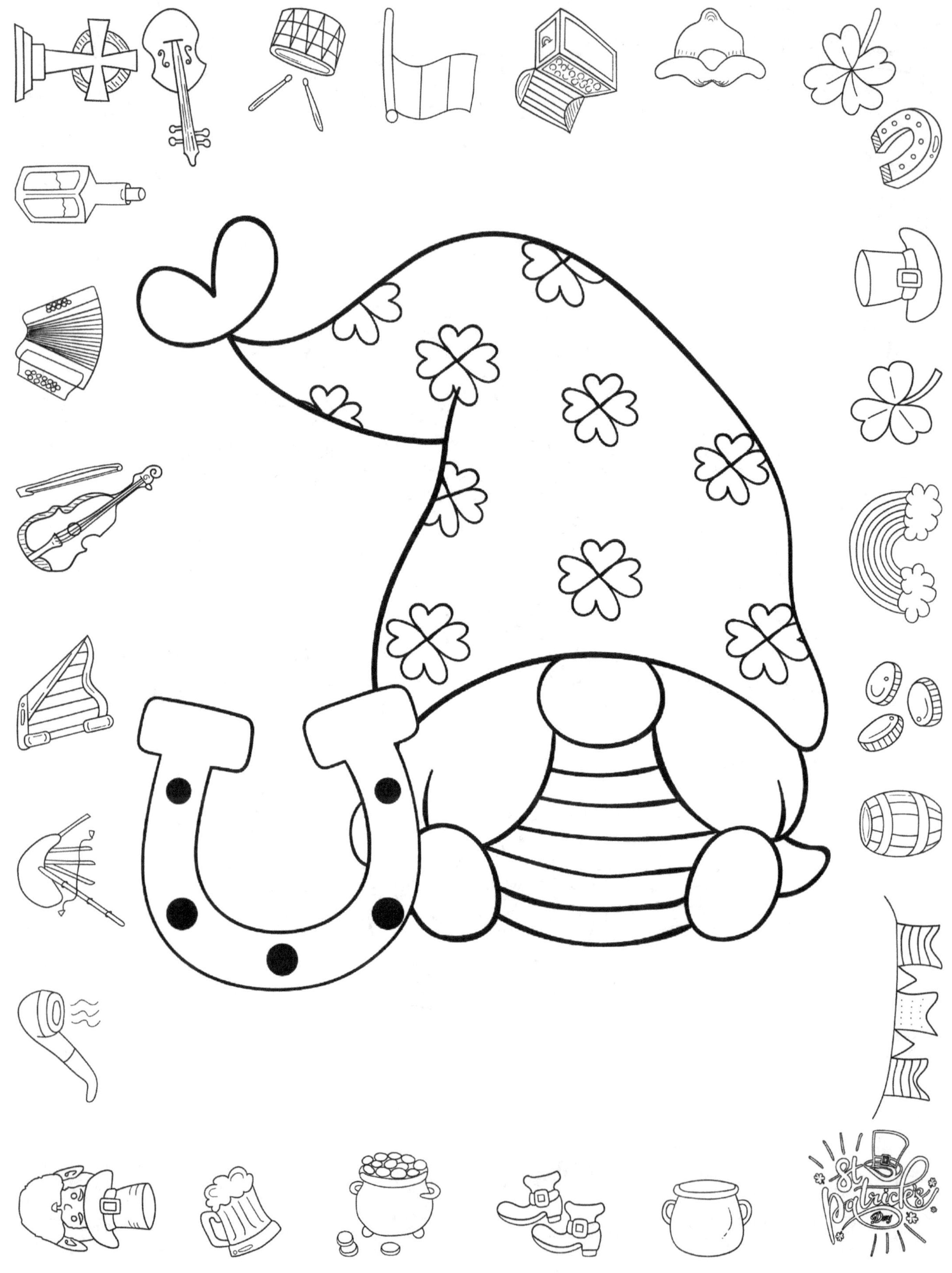

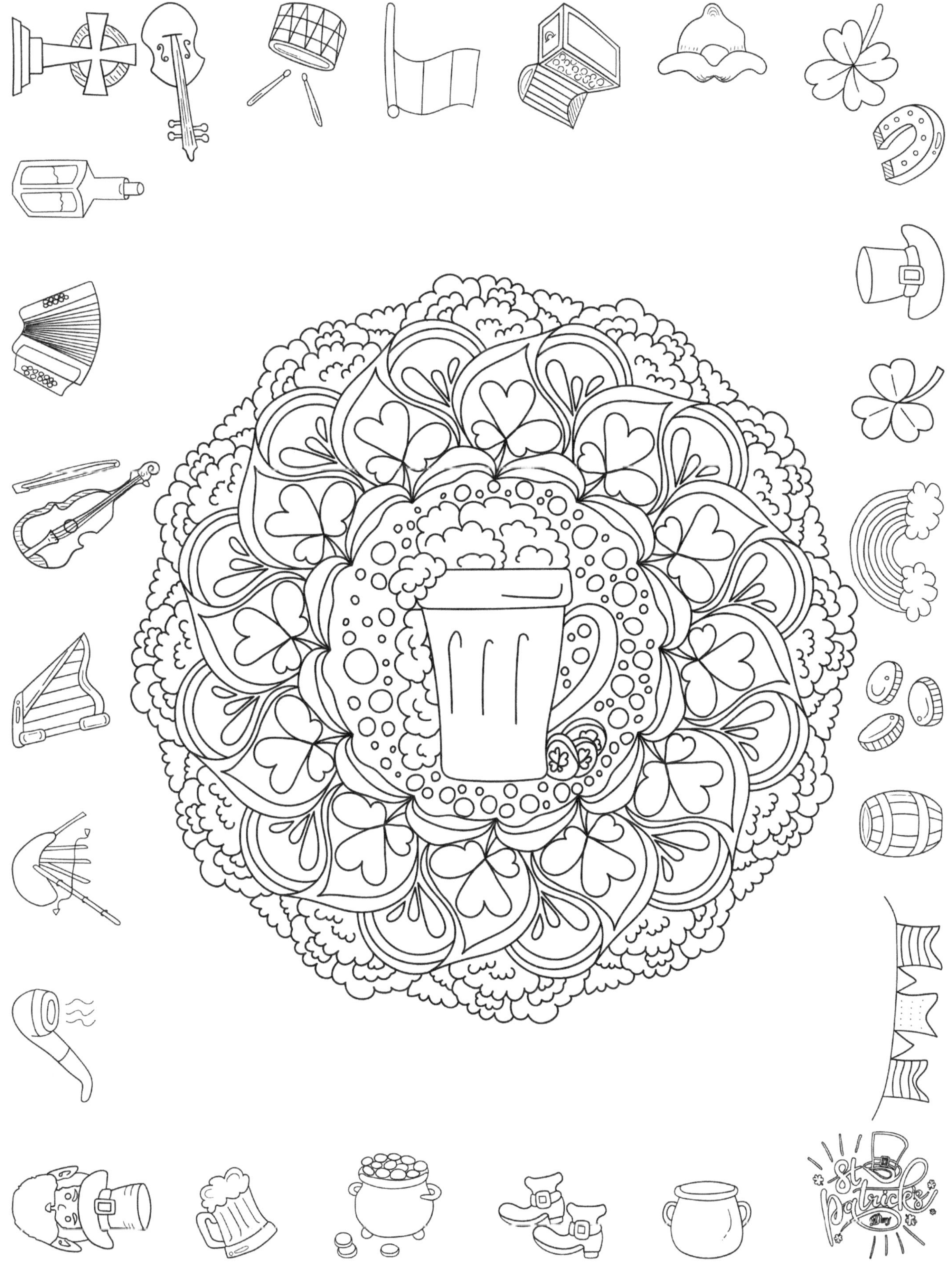

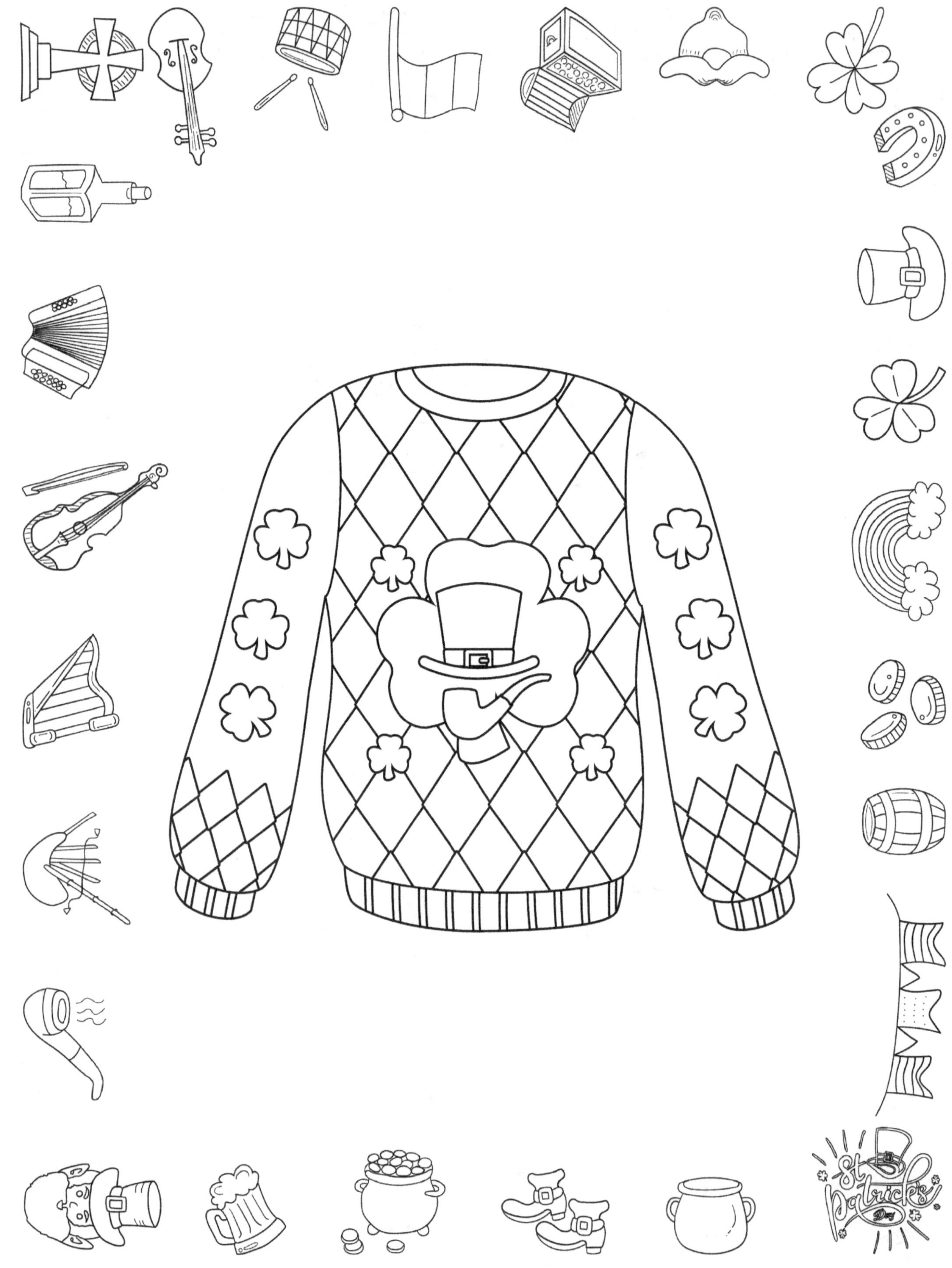

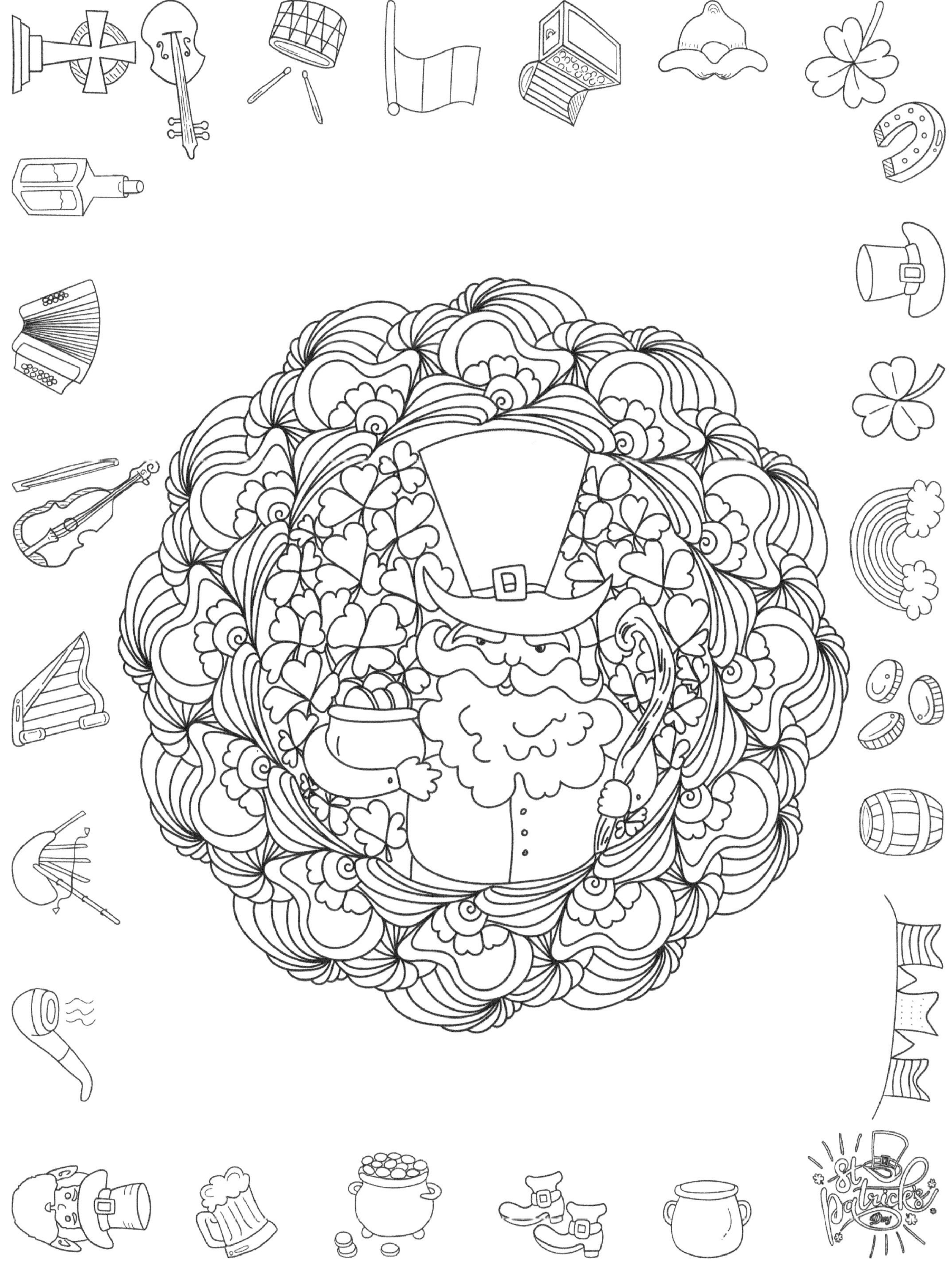

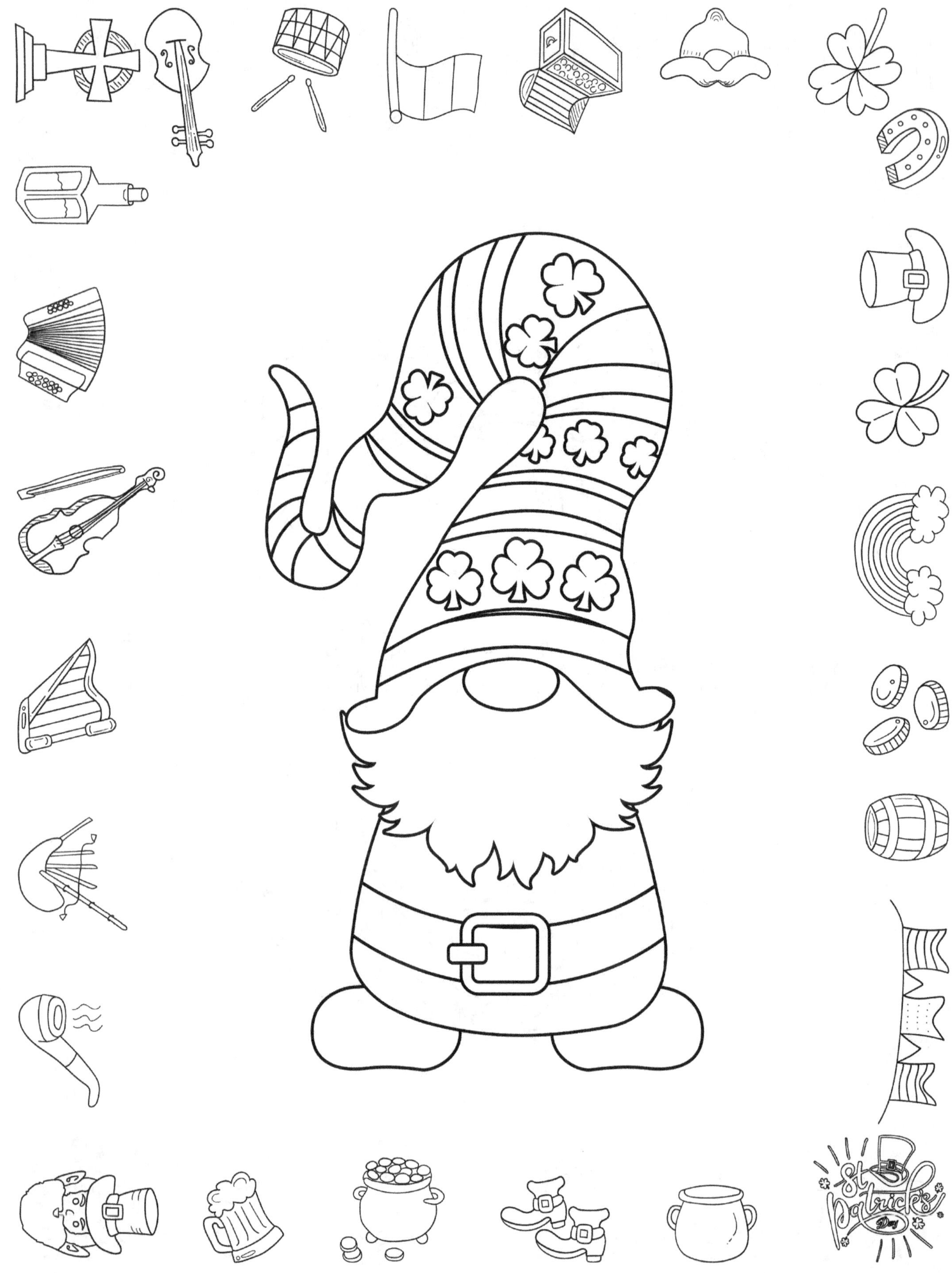

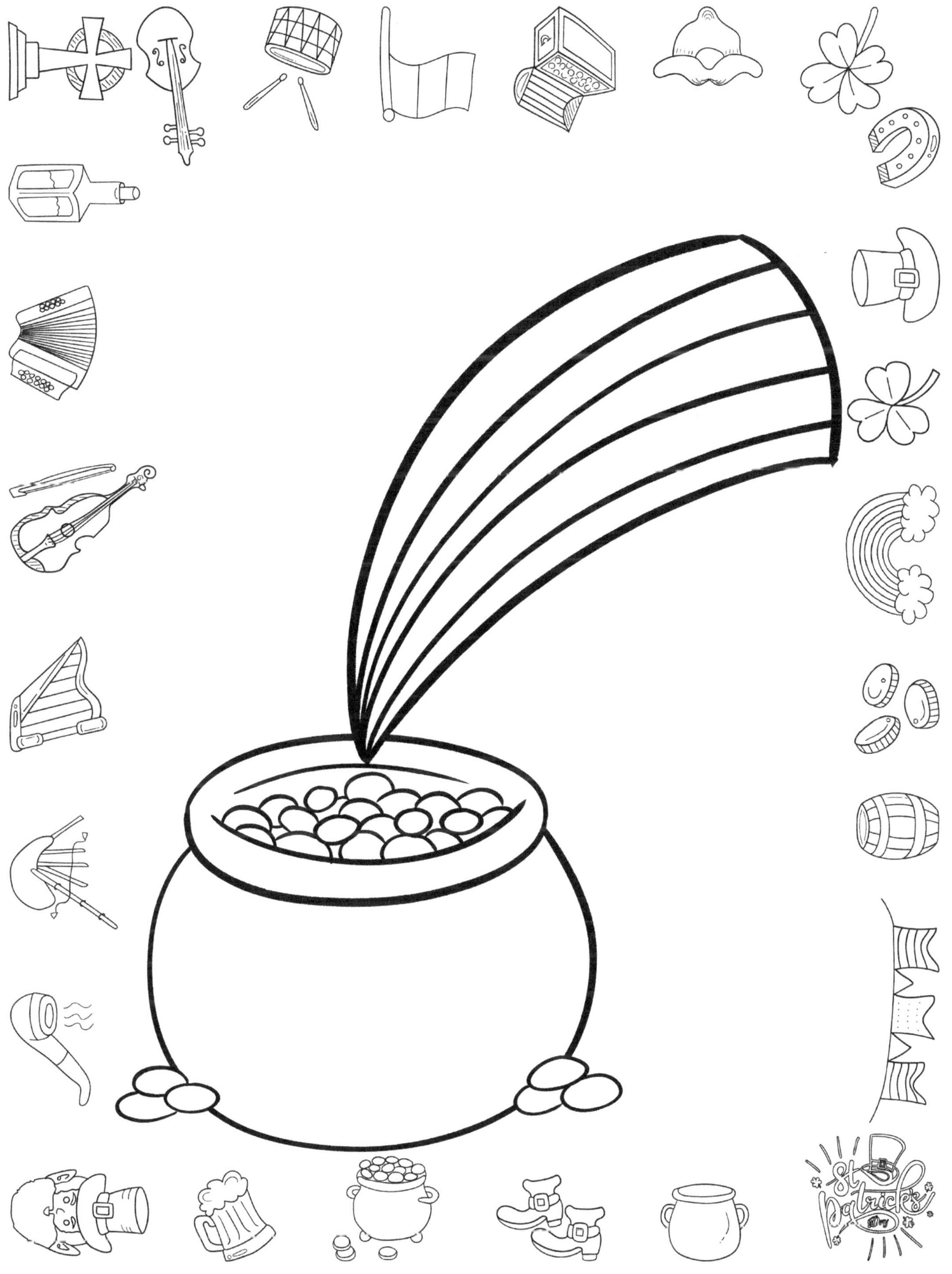

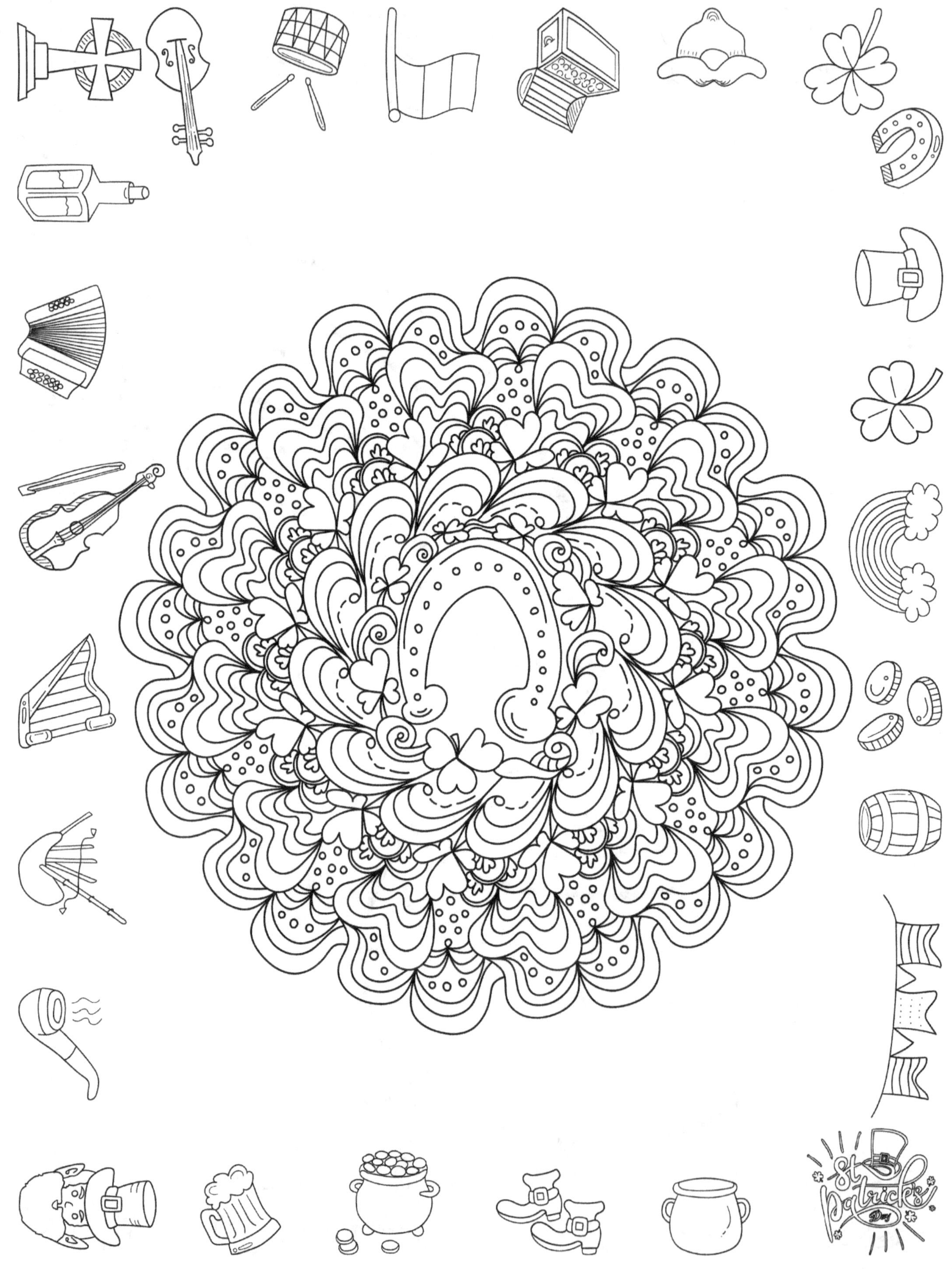

St Patrick's Day

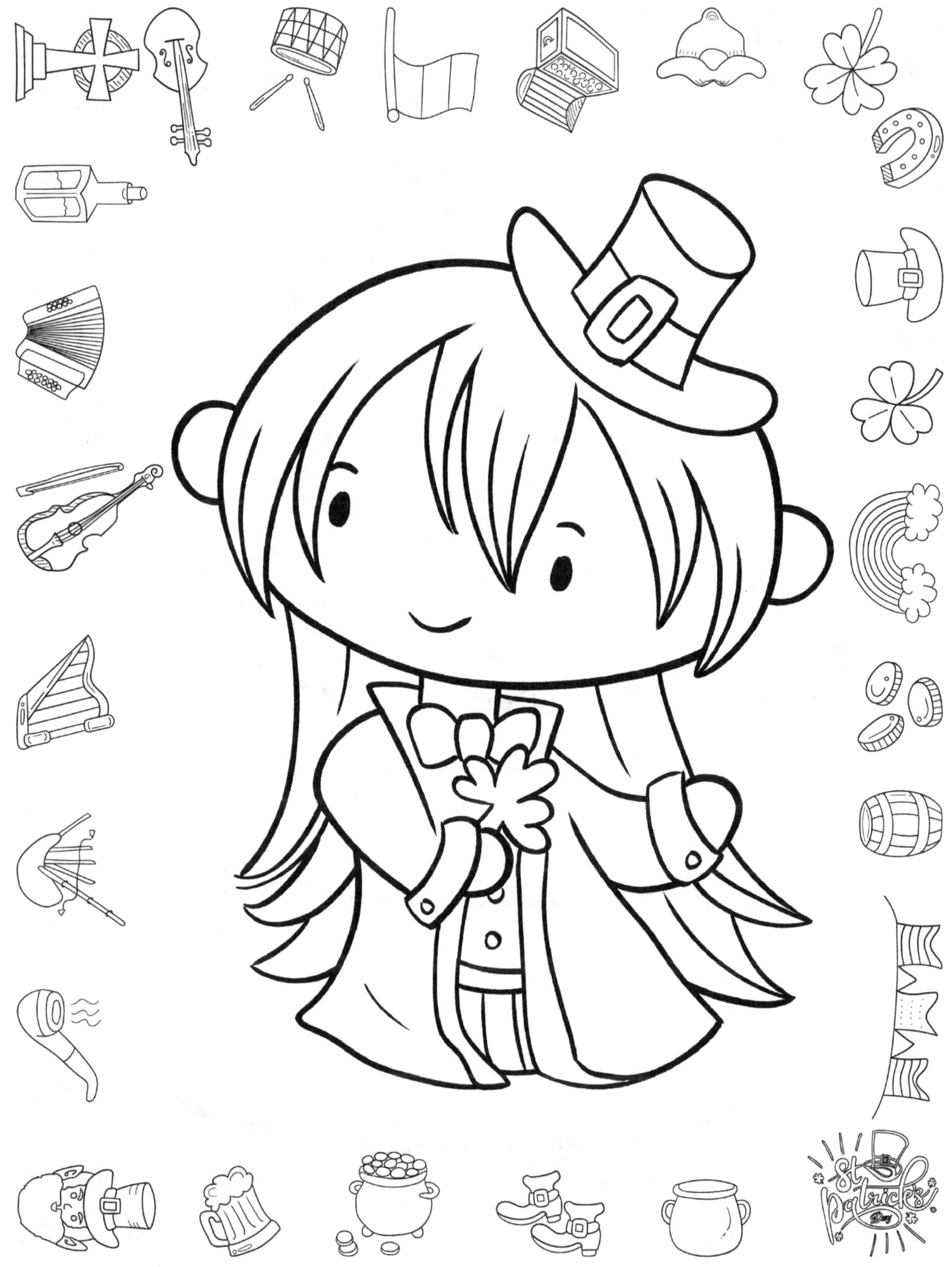

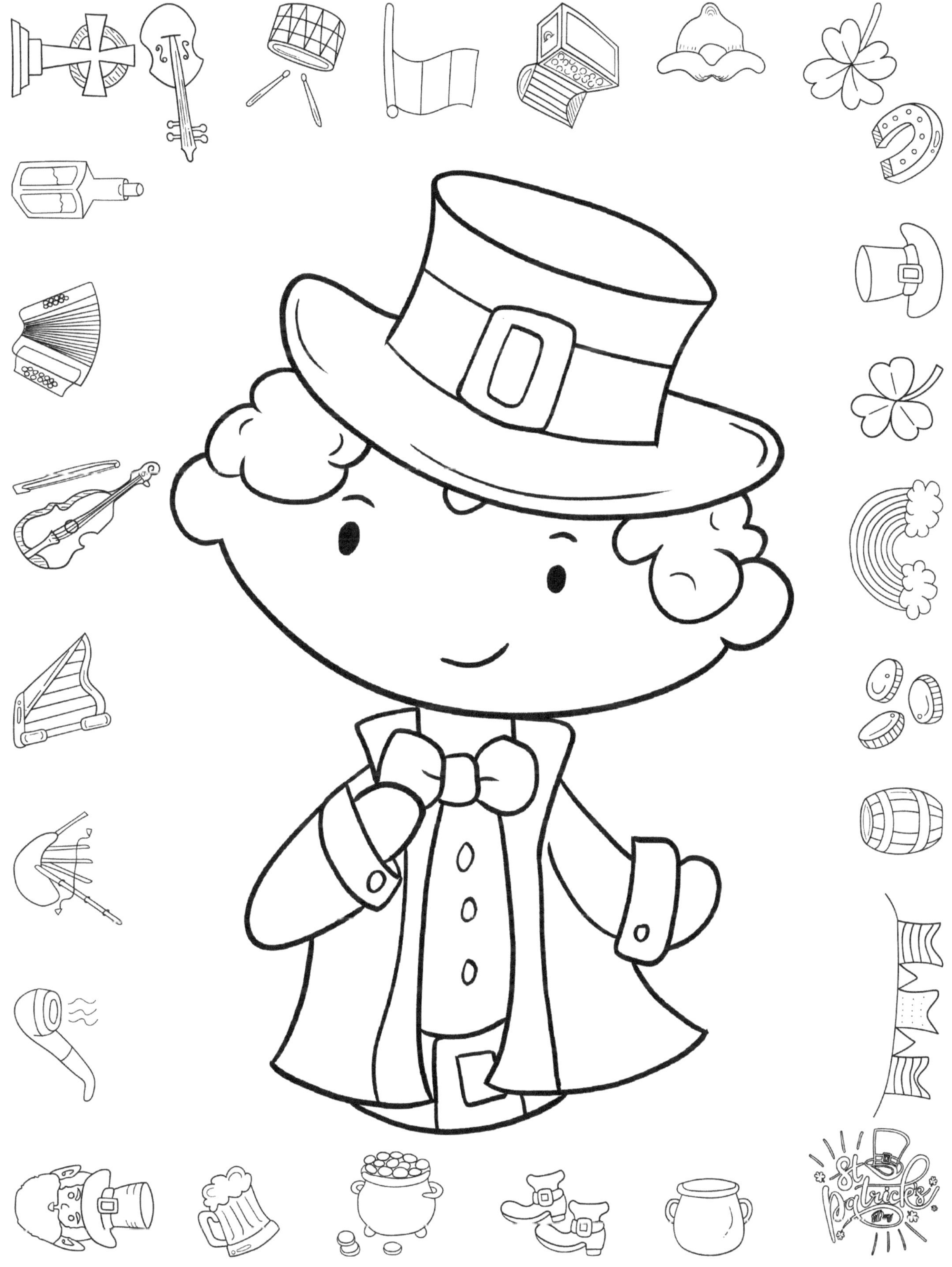

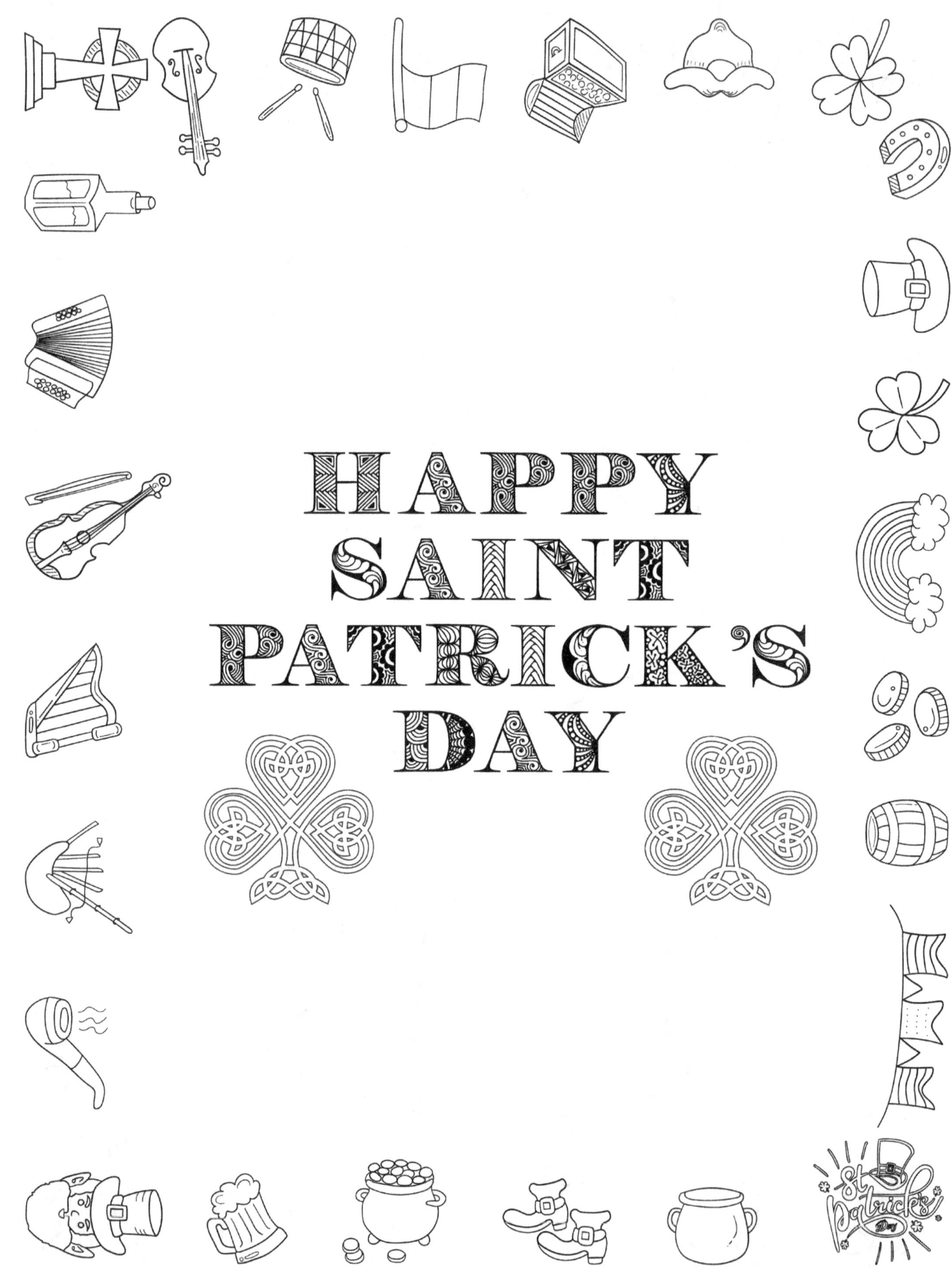

HAPPY
SAINT
PATRICK'S
DAY

Be on the lookout
for our other
Big Coloring Book
Titles!
Check our author
page on Amazon at:

https://www.amazon.com/Journals-ForYou/e/B08SDWYPJ3